THE BIBLE
and THE FAMILY

THE AUTHOR

HAZEN G. WERNER is a bishop of The Methodist Church assigned to the Taiwan-Hong-Kong area. He is chairman of the Methodist World Family Life Committee and was chairman of the Family Life Commission of The Methodist Church from 1948 to 1964. He has participated in family life conferences in 14 foreign countries during that time.

Bishop Werner is a graduate of Albion College (B.A.) and Drew Theological Seminary (B.D.). He has been awarded numerous honorary degrees. He served pastorates in Michigan and Ohio before accepting the chair in practical theology at Drew, where he was teaching when elected a bishop in 1948 and assigned to the Ohio area.

He is the author of *No Saints Suddenly, Christian Family Living,* and *Real Living Takes Time,* all published by Abingdon Press.

THE BIBLE
and THE FAMILY

HAZEN G. WERNER

ABINGDON PRESS
NASHVILLE
NEW YORK

THE BIBLE AND THE FAMILY

Copyright © 1966 by Abingdon Press

Library of Congress Catalog Card Number: 66-22915

SET UP, PRINTED, AND BOUND BY THE
PARTHENON PRESS, AT NASHVILLE,
TENNESSEE, UNITED STATES OF AMERICA

✤

For children across the world who have won our hearts

PREFACE

Two interests occupy these pages, marriage and family life, and what the Scriptures say about them. The family is the veteran institution of man's history. It began with creation. The whole earth was made for man and woman related to parenthood; a world in which to rear their young and nurture the mind and body of their offspring.

This book grew out of three studies given at Bangkok in February of 1964 in the Consultation on the Church and Parental Responsibilities, held under the auspices of the East Asia Council of Churches.

Other sources for the understanding of the family as the basic unit for society are utilized here, but the Bible will be our chief reference. The word of God throws important light on marriage and family life, their mission and destiny. Particularly rich in contemporary insights are the new translations such as the Revised Standard Version, Moffatt's translation, the New English Bible, and Phillips' translation.

Since the family is as old as the beginning of time, we turn to the divine record of that beginning. We are using the Bible as a basic resource because of the wisdom that we find in it about family life. The view that the meaning of man, of marriage, and of parenthood, inlays all of life, as a constituent part of life from its beginning, finds ample support in scriptural and theological truth. When you start out to know all you can about what the Bible has to say concerning man, marriage, and the family, you discover the abundance of references to these subjects.

According to one author, the first duty of a writer is to protect the reader from boredom. The Bible is a tremendously alive book. "For the word of God is alive and active. It cuts more keenly than any two-edged sword." (Heb. 4:12 NEB.) Pointing to a copy of the Bible on the mantle, Karl Barth once said to a student, "Of course I believe that the Bible is the Word of God. But I will also say that that Bible will not become the Word of God to any person until that person takes the Bible off the mantle and makes it a part of his mind and heart."

In work of this sort it will not do to embellish one's ideas about the home with some scriptural verses that seem to have some relation to what is discussed. You can't get yourself equipped with the correct biblical phrases and then go forth to do battle for monogamy or proper child discipline. The deeper ministry of the Bible in reference to the family is to enlighten men and women regarding the relationships of the home, and what in those relationships is consonant with God's will and spirit. The Bible lights up the whole marital and family scene. It does this often without using either term. "The New Testament," said John Jowett, "does not say very much about homes, it says a great deal about things that make them."

In other words turn to the Scriptures to understand that it is from God that "every family in heaven and on earth derives its name and nature" (Eph. 3:14-15 Moffatt).

HAZEN G. WERNER

CONTENTS

1. IMAGE 11

2. MAN 19

3. MARRIAGE 31

4. PARENTS 51

5. FAMILY 61

6. MOTHERS AND FATHERS 74

7. CHILDREN 84

8. HOUSE 97

9. SPIRIT 104

✤
1. IMAGE

All the rich and grievous things of home life are used, in the Scriptures, to symbolize the relation of the divine to the human. The love, the laughter, the pensive moment, the regrettable disloyalty, the bowed heart of bereavement—all these experiences, probable and sometimes inevitable, within the life of the family, are pictorially lifted up by scriptural writers to mirror the life of God with his people. The confiding, assuring relation of father and son is plainly revealed in the word of Jesus, "No man knoweth the Son, but the father; neither knoweth any man the Father, save the Son" (Matt. 11:27 KJV). Further, the very nature of the Trinity implies the kind of relationship that is best illustrated by the structure of the family. The Trinity—three in one—dynamic and profound is seen in the life together of father, mother, and child. The innocence of a little child is used by the Master to explain the meaning of conversion. "Unless you turn round and become like children, you will never enter the kingdom of Heaven." (Matt. 18:3 NEB.)

Marriage and family life are used to help us understand the way in which God is related to us. The solicitude for a sick one, the faithfulness till death, the sacrificial love of one family member for the other—these and other analogies are widely employed to make clear the truth of divine concern and affection.

There is metaphorical power in the use of these images. A

11

metaphor or figure of speech conveys a meaning more completely than paragraphs of description. By the distillation of meaning into a single picture a truth is carried to the understanding clearly and instantly—instant realization. One of the remarkable features of the Gospels is Jesus' continuous use of terms that pictorially convey his message to his listeners. His parables are actually expanded metaphors. What a wealth of truth, what succinct lessons about life, Jesus gives us in the parables of the sower, of the prodigal son, of the laborers in the vineyard, of the five wise virgins. Note also how completely and simply Isaiah interpreted God's feeling for his people in the words, "As the bridegroom rejoices over the bride, so shall your God rejoice over you" (Isa. 62:5).

Marriage as a symbol of God in relation to his people and of Christ in relation to the church is found everywhere throughout the Bible. God injured by the desertion of a believer is pictured as a dejected wife who has been deserted by her husband, "for the Lord has called you like a wife forsaken and grieved in spirit" (Isa. 54:6). A marriage in which the beauty and loveliness that once held a husband and wife together are now only a memory has God speaking to Israel, "I remember the devotion of your youth, your love as a bride" (Jer. 2:2). The relation to God is pictured here as worn through like a threadbare marriage. Hosea uses married love as a symbol of God's patience and his merciful feeling concerning the people of Israel.

Early Christian writers spoke of Christians as comprising God's family. The church was the family of God. Paul speaks of the Lord as saying, "I will be a father to you, and you shall be my sons and daughters" (II Cor. 6:18). He admonishes

12

the Ephesians, "Husbands, love your wives, as Christ loved the church and gave himself up for her" (Eph. 5:25).

Speaking further on the subject to the Ephesians, Paul says, "For this reason a man shall leave his father and mother and be joined to his wife, and the two shall become one." He continues, "This is a great mystery, and I take it to mean Christ and the church; however, let each one of you love his wife as himself, and let the wife see that she respects her husband" (Eph. 5:31-33).

It is interesting to note that, while man was made in the image of God, much that we find in the Scriptures presenting God and his relation to us is in the imagery of man. The apt and true simile making clear Christ's complete self-giving presents him as the bridegroom—a bridegroom willing to lay down his life for his bride.

Reasons for Use of These Images

The widespread use of familial imagery in the Scriptures is grounded unmistakably in the fact that marriage and parenthood were considered supremely vital. The authors of our Judeo-Christian writing employed these metaphors of marriage and family relations because they knew of no better way to make evident that rich and meaningful relation of the divine with the human. For one thing the imagery of marriage and family life could never lose its relevance. It would be hard to think of a time when a father's care, a wife's fidelity, or a child's obedience would not have profound and lasting meaning. Further reason for the use of these symbols of marriage and the family is that universally man can under-

13

stand them. They are not the symbols of a negligible or secondary part of life. The plain man can understand them. The Scripture is talking his language. Since families are universal, everyone knows what the Scripture is talking about when it uses the terms "bride," "bridegroom," "widow," "husband," "father," "children." These images are warm, living, and self-interpreting.

There is an artistry about all of this. "The symbol is not a mere quotation of speech," says Richard Niebuhr. "Symbol and reality participate in each other." Marriage and family life became the imagery for two kinds of reality: the commonplace social and domestic experiences of all of us, and on the other hand the meaning of the covenant of God with his people.

Basically, the richness of these anthropomorphisms is to be found in the fact that the hallowed experience of family life resembles most the holy experiences of relation to God. This truth came home to the writer as he listened to Dean Mathews, in a message in St. Paul's Cathedral, speak of the last supper as a family meal. He linked the communion table with the family dinner table.

Note also that the Bible uses the home of man to depict the home of his soul. "There are many dwelling-places in my Father's house." (John 14:2 NEB.) What greater reward for the faithful than to dwell in our Father's home evermore? In her novel *The Dean's Watch* Elizabeth Goudge has the Dean saying to Isaac, "And it is a house not made with hands." He continues, "Yet when our play is ended and the house lights go up we shall see many kindly faces. It is a house, remember, a friendly place."

THE TERM "FATHER"

One of the most commonly used familial terms in the Bible is that of "father." In the New Testament one has the feeling that the elements of the human and divine meet together in a transcending reality in the use that Jesus made of this term. In only a restricted number of instances did he speak of God as the Father, but each time he spoke the word with warmth and meaning. For Jesus the term "father" was expressive of tenderness and intimacy. He used the expression "Abba Father" (Mark 14:36 KJV). William Barclay tells us that "abba" is a word a young child would use to address his father. To Jesus, "Father" summed up all that he came to say about God to man.

His use of the term "father" to make clear God's relation to his people has its own fascination. An earthly father is symbolic of the heavenly Father—or should be. The instances of compassion and protective concern of an earthly father become clues to the loving care of the heavenly Father. "Or what man of you, if his son asks him for a loaf, will give him a stone? Or if he asks for a fish, will give him a serpent? If you then, who are evil, know how to give good gifts to your children, how much more will your Father who is in heaven give good things to those who ask him?" (Matt. 7:9, 10.)

Being a father is an awesome responsibility. The word "father" may mean no more than the designation of the person who has given life to a child, or the term may connote father as a parent, related to a child in both understanding and love.

A FAMILY LIKENESS

With a slight turning of the idea of the family symbol you have a somewhat different use for this term as found in the Scriptures. In marriage and in family life man is expected to achieve a kind of "likeness" in terms of character and conduct of the highest order. What kind of likeness? The sacredness of marriage and of family relations had its beginning in Genesis when God said, "Let us make man in our image, after our likeness" (Gen. 1:26). This same divine expectancy concerning man in all his intimate relations makes its way through Old Testament prophecy, legalism, and history. There is to be a likeness, a resemblance, a similarity, in the life of the home to the life of the infinite. Paul seemed to think so. To the Galatians he declared, "All of you who were baptized 'into' Christ have put on the family likeness of Christ" (Gal. 3:27 Phillips). Interestingly enough the New English Bible reads "put on Christ as a garment," and the Moffatt translation reads "taken on the character of Christ."

There is a basis for a "family likeness" in Jesus' life and work. It is found in his background of experiences with people. His "family likeness" was grounded in the realism of those experiences. He was born into a family. The first thirty years of his life were spent in close relations with his own family. Throughout the silent years, William Barclay tells us, "Jesus was learning the meaning of family life." He noted the strained relations of Martha and Mary in their home, the differences of temperament causing the tension between them; he shared in the grief over Lazarus' death; he felt the deep hurt of little children, their sensitivities wounded by the stumbling blocks

16

of adult life around them; he experienced the pain of a father's heart whose son had gone his prodigal way.

There came a time when his own relations to his family were strained to the breaking point. At the outset of his career his family, together with many of the people in the community, could not go along with his thinking. The common conclusion was that Jesus was mad. Finally his family, mother and brothers, appeared on the scene to take him home—John says, "For even his brothers did not believe in him" (John 7:5). There are times when, as Jesus said, "a man's foes will be those of his own household" (Matt. 10:36). All this and more Jesus came to experience. And yet to him marriage and family life were most sacred. It was of these living relations that there accrued in the mind and nature of Jesus a "likeness" that has a marked pertinency here.

Marriage and the home are to take on the "likeness," "the character of Christ." Is this the validity of the marriage vow "till death us do part"? Is this the explanation of the fact that while divorce can be legalized, rationalized, normalized, there remains still a strange immutability about a consummated union in marriage? A marriage is not just a contract, a ceremony, a legal compliance; a marriage is a blending of two lives in such a spiritual way that they can never be wholly unblended.

If we believe this, then we would agree that marriage and the family are timeless. There is something ultimate about them. A clever journalist, says Edmond Bergler in his book (which by the way has a significant title—*Divorce Won't Help*), once called marriage a "two dimensional study in frustration, an intimate relation without intimacy." If this cynical judgment is true, then men and women in our society are more sick than we know.

Most of us sense something of the incomprehensible in marriage. We don't know what it is, we cannot define it or put our finger on its source. We have a feeling that marriage has an almost unfathomable depth in spite of the fact that many make it a shallow matter. We feel further that marriage and the family relation should move us toward the highest character of love and loyalty or else they fail their appointed use.

This view finds support in Paul's word to the Ephesians, "For this reason, then, I kneel before the Father from whom every family in heaven and on earth derives its name and nature" (Eph. 3:14-15 Moffatt). Here is the charter for the divine nature of our homes—a charter written large in responsibilities of our homes that stirs us to strive to take on "the character of Christ."

For marriage and the family to dwell and function on this high level is a large order. But a Christian home can attempt no less. We need to remind ourselves that a Christian home is not a secular home and certainly not a pagan home, but a home where there is a proper climate for a child's spiritual growth, an ethical life in keeping with the teachings of Jesus and a daily fellowship with God in prayer.

✢
2. MAN

Through exploration in the fifteenth and sixteenth centuries man acquired some knowledge of the world round about him. By the nineteenth century he had come to possess a fairly reliable grasp of the nature of matter, as well as the laws of the universe. In the middle of that century a man by the name of Freud began to shed some light on the inner life—the unconscious life of man. As one person observed, "It was a cold North light. There was neither peace in it nor mercy." You may not like Freud or anything about him, but he did start man questioning. Man's curiosity was aroused about the psychological nature of a human being. Man began to ask, "What am I really like?" "What does my life mean?" In the meantime psychology with its new and experimental insights, on its way to becoming a science, has furnished considerable help in the understanding of man.

Earlier in this history of the study of the self Plato had been asking, "What does it mean to be a man?" Man is still asking that question. In fact we are asking it right here. At the end of Arthur Miller's play, *Death of a Salesman,* Biff says about Willy Loman, the central character of the drama, "He never knew who he was." Who does? But we had better try. The late Don Marquis imagined a message coming through from Mars following the establishment of communication with Earth: "We are creatures inhabiting a planet—who cannot agree what they are or where they came from, or where they are going to." One person commenting on this suggested that Earth would flash back: "Same here." Such an exchange of messages would certainly leave us with the question, what is man like? You will never know the meaning of man in his relations to marriage and the family until you know something of the meaning and nature of man himself.

SELF-UNDERSTANDING

Alfred Adler seemed to think this important. "Self-understanding," he said, "is the first law of happiness." Perhaps Paul was bothered by this need. In fact he indicated to the Corinthians the way in which he thought this self-understanding was to be achieved. "Among men," he said, "who knows what man is but the man's own spirit within him" (I Cor. 2:11 NEB). So it is every man's job to understand himself. What is he like? What does he mean in the venture of existence? Be sure of one thing, that whatever man is meant to be will not be understood aside from his essential human nature; these throbbing, devouring, demanding feelings inside a person. The meaning of marriage and the meaning of the family rest back upon the nature as well as the meaning of a person.

THE MEANING OF MAN

Turn then, concerning the meaning of man, to the important resources that are found in the Scriptures. The dimension as well as the pertinence of man's meaning await our exegetical understanding of what is said in the Old and New Testaments at this point. These truths are implicit in the Creation narrative as found in Genesis: (1) Man came into being in the likeness of God. (2) Man was intended to be the highest order of life. (3) Man was meant to live in fruitful relations. The glorious achievement of all creation was man. Not the fish of the sea, not the fowl of the air, not the fruit of the field, but man is the great phenomenon of creation's grandeur. God said, "Let us make man in our image, after our likeness" (Gen. 1:26). Out of that moment of solemn cosmic climax man was born. Man's high meaning derives from God alone. In the sense of being a person man was born in the image of God, in the sense of the attributes of personality, man was born in his likeness. Herein is the glory of man, that God made him like himself. We are told that Thomas Carlyle once cried out to a congress of biologists, "Gentlemen, make man a little higher than a tadpole. I believe with the ancient Psalmist who said, 'Thou has made him a little less than God.'"

It is this divine eminence of man, his God-given meaning, that has become a keystone principle of political and economic philosophy. The dignity and meaning of man take on added significance in the light of Jesus. He was a man like all men, and, since he was, he forever placed on man the mark of eternal worth. We have built our culture on this great truth. Our political institutions, our social services, our economic structure, voice our belief in the dignity and worth of man, but our practices deny and destroy this sacred meaning.

MATERIALISM AND MAN

In the Western world materialism is creating man in its own image. This image gives him the value of a purchasing potential. The meaning of the individual is seen in terms of his purchasing power—a consumerism in which more and more we exist to buy. We in America are increasing our gross national income and at the same time our bondage. The consumer is caught in a vicious squeeze. The advertising tools of our economy leave no part of our lives, our privacy, our consciousness, unexplored or unexploited. The result is sinister depersonalization. To this low level the human being has descended. Modern commercialism was made articulate in the words of Sir Herbert Lawrence of Vicers Arms Corporation, when he said that "the sanctity of human life has been exaggerated." Look at the way in which John Smith has been numeralized. The day of the digit is upon us. Halford Luccock once wrote of a slave woman who stood watching General Sherman's army marching by—endlessly. Her comment was, "I reckon they ain't all got names." We have names, but we are about to be robbed of them. In the present frenzy to digitize everyone, someone has suggested that the telephone company give each child at birth a telephone number, and in turn this would serve through life to identify this person for the purposes of Social Security, "the use of insurance agents, bank inspectors, tax collectors, and postal authorities—a name of course would be unnecessary." We are told that Noel Coward once wrote to T. E. Lawrence, "Dear 338171 (May I call you 338?)."

You can't bring back the day of the party line, the fringed

surrey, gaslights, nor the warm and wondrous gift of neigh-bors. But let it be said that one number or a series of numbers representing a human being certainly will not help preserve his sense of meaning or, for that matter, his self-respect. Num-eralism is making man nameless, faceless, and meaningless.

In a certain sense this hypermaterialistic kind of life has resulted in a culture primitive in its passions and its low level of concerns, and in a society of persons literate but tough. Life is cast in a new setting, greatly dressed up, but with more of the old evils. Man who was meant to aim at the stars is not getting much farther than the street lamp. There is no greater imperative than the recapture of the dignity and integrity God meant man to have and along with these to know again some of the simple graces of family devotion that give mean-ing to life. Perhaps worst of all is that the man of the '60s is not aware of how far he has gone in moral and spiritual decline. What has been sacrificed is reality.

Life in this modern, materialistic, impersonal setting is il-lusion. We might as well look for nourishment in confetti. "Happiness is Channel 2," a voice on T.V. instructs us. Ac-cording to one columnist, "On any channel these fetid nights one could learn the art of exchanging a few pennies for de-lirium." There are at least two brands of cigarettes which promise unalloyed Nirvana. On the screen appear mindless teenagers who inhale, then turn and display their teeth to one another in transports of delight. Automobiles are alleged to thrill you with their taillights. Refrigerators have the power to make whole families quiver with pleasure at their enlarged freezer compartments. Arnold Toynbee, commenting on the T.V. situation under the title, "The Lion That Squeaks," talked about "the prostitution of this product of mature human genius to soothe childish tastes." He went on to say, "If the viewers would stop viewing such inferior stuff, I am sure that commercial self-interest would push the purveyors into giving their customers something better." In all of this meaninglessness we find some basis for the otherwise senseless eruptions of youth across the world. These young people may not understand themselves—may not fully grasp their own inner revulsions at the phoniness of our adult culture. Note that now you can hire a demonstrator who will march in the interest of any cause—paid for by the hour. "Now your town can have a professional riot." This is the announcement of Demonstrators, Inc. The statement continues, "Ninety days advance notice will be needed to guarantee spontaneity." The sheer emptiness of life is turning our youth toward nihilism. They have decided to go us one better. It is all right for Carlyle Marney to say that "nihilism is for sophomores" but nihilism is not for anyone unless we wish for our common spiritual death—for the destruction of order and the complete wiping out of the meaning of man.

Man is created in the image of God, in his likeness. We have an immense job on our hands to restore in man that imagery. The Christian faith can restore man to what originally he was meant to be—born in God's image and in his likeness—restore the integrity of his original significance. This is his right.

Man's Earthiness

Turn to the second Genesis account for the picture of creation. "And the Lord God formed man of the dust of the ground, and breathed into his nostrils the breath of life; and man became a living soul." (2:7 KJV.) From the dust of the ground—a living soul. This second account of creation makes unmistakable the earthiness of man. While man is a living soul he is also a biological being with all the attending hungers of his human nature.

THE BIBLE AND HUMAN NATURE

What can we find out biblically about human nature? To begin with, the Scriptures come alive with it. This is because they are filled with the truth about human beings. The Bible is not a picture book, not an album of sentimental journeys; it tells the objective truth about what man is like. Herein is much of its greatness. The infantilism of Ahab who, sulking, went to bed, turning his face to the wall because a neighbor refused his offer for a piece of land; the wall-builder, the great Nehemiah, demanding credit for every achievement; the feeling of inferiority showing through every word of the young Hebrews who, returning from their spying in Canaan, reported, "We were in our sight as grasshoppers and so were we in their sight." This is human nature—in its weakness and its strength. The story of emotional change for good is seen in the history of Moses who, hotheaded as a youth, became immortalized as an example of meekness; John, one of the sons of thunder, who in his last days was heard to admonish his people, "Little children, love one another." The strong and the weak, the good and the bad, in all their realism vividly illustrating man's human nature, are to be found in the Scriptures.

In the New Testament we meet the belief of Jesus that man's emotional life could and would be identified with the highest ends. John said of Jesus, "Well did he know what was in human nature." Here is one of the genuinely great facts of the gospel, Jesus believed that man caught in the welter of his own desires could triumph.

The New Testament record makes clear that one of the great things about human nature is its redeemability. In all the problems involving man's emotional life Jesus never lost heart. Man can be raised to the shining likeness of God; the earthy creature can be made new in the glory of a new birth. This is the overarching theme of the New Testament. Jesus believed in the recoverability of man at his worst.

Human Nature Potential

The fact basic to all our discussion about human nature is that it is not fixed or rigid but potential. William E. Hocking in his book *Human Nature and Its Remaking* not only provides the key to the understanding of what is basic in human nature but his position coincides with what is basic in Jesus' faith in man. "There is nothing in human nature," this philosopher-psychologist said, "that taken by itself can be called evil. To anyone who asserts as a dogma that human nature never changes, it is fair to reply 'it is human nature to change itself.'" He goes on to say, "As to structure human nature is undoubtedly the most plastic part of the living world, most adaptable, most educable."

Human nature is neither good nor bad. Good and bad are the final forms of behavior resulting from good or bad conditioning. Ashley Montagu observes, "What most persons have taken to be human nature is actually acquired behavior of the person."

Based upon this second creation account in Genesis, man is born earthly and spiritual—born of the dust of the earth—yet a living soul. Christians early held to the doctrine of dualism. Actually, body and spirit are not hostile but complementary one to the other. Human nature is neither inherently nor inevitably evil. If human nature is essentially evil then humanity is caught in an immense cosmic trap, but Jesus challenges us with the command, "Be ye therefore perfect, even as your Father which is in heaven is perfect" (Matt. 5:48 KJV). Surely he is not mocking us. Human beings are not destined to sin. They are, however, conditioned to a tendency to sin. Paul speaks of "sin which has made its home within me" (Rom. 7:20 Phillips). But even the tendency to sin does not condemn us to sin. Only as man holds a spiritual disciplining power over his emotional life will he have true freedom in regard to his human nature.

SEX EDUCATION

Sex education is not proving the cure-all for our modern moral decadence that we had hoped. In our zeal to disarm the old ugly concepts and dispel the fears and guilt feelings of the young we have given the impression that adequate knowledge is the complete liberator. But even adequate knowledge is not a solution. In an attempt to normalize thinking about sex we have talked ourselves back into the very problem we have been trying to resolve. No farmer burns down his barn to get rid of the mice. Ernest van den Haage observes that "today's manuals are produced not by men of letters but by doctors and therapists as though love, sex and marriage were diseases or therapeutic problems which they promptly become if one reads too many of these guide books (any one is too many). The authors are sure that happiness depends on the sexual mechanics they blueprint."

It is scripturally written into the creation charter that man is to have dominion over all nature. After the creation of the sea, the earth, vegetation, animal life—the whole physical, biological world—

Then God said, "Let us make man in our image, after our likeness; and let them have dominion over the fish of the sea, and over the birds of the air, and over the cattle, and over all the earth, and over every creeping thing that creeps upon the earth." So God created man in his own image, in the image of God he created him; male and female he created them. And God blessed them, and God said to them, "Be fruitful and multiply, and fill the earth and subdue it; and have dominion over . . . every living thing that moves upon the earth" (Gen. 1:26-28).

While man was created as a part of the whole physical life, he was destined to transcend it—to rise above it. Man is more than an organism. In our desire to get rid of outworn views on sex we have forgotten the basic, the healthy, thinking about it as part of man's spiritual mission; without this integration with the spiritual life sex loses its integrity. Too much of the talk about sex on the part of religious leaders is devoid of sacredness. We are dispelling the mystery so much a part of its beauty and loveliness. The growing child must come to know about sex, but not all about it all at once. You don't read the whole book to him just because he has asked a question, any more than you confront him with higher algebra when he is just beginning simple arithmetic. He must come to know, but it must be the kind of knowing that does not increase the hazards of self-involvement. Certainly one of the strong implications of the creation truth is that man is meant to exercise dominion over the physical world and not be overcome by it. There must enter into all impartation the element of spiritual responsibility and certainly of wholesome wonder and development. One of the recent positions that sexual life has been given to us not only for procreation but also for the enrichment and deepening of the lives of the two people concerned in a marital experience certainly makes sex education imperative, as a spiritual venture. We must teach that which will lift up the whole of man; herein is the integrity of the situation.

In the chronology of creation the earthiness of man was not his last state. Man became a living soul.

Man Exists Only in Relations

Note the sequel to this creation account. Man derives his meaning from others, from relationships. The Lord said, "It is not good that man should be alone." Man is by nature social. He is a being who was created for communication with others. The source of creativity is to be found in the meaning of man as active in relations with other persons. A member of the party that scaled Mount Everest observed, "No one climbs alone." This is axiomatic. There is much to substantiate the thesis that man exists only in relation to others. It was Paul Tournier who said, "What creates in one the consciousness of being a person is entering into a relationship with another person."

In respect to this need of relations marriage offers the most complete answer. The response to our deepest needs—the need to belong, to be loved and to love, to be important, to be needed—the response to these hungers is to be found in the intimate relations of marriage that have brought about the priceless enrichments that make up much of the fulfillment of one's person.

"Then the Lord God said, 'It is not good that man should be alone; I will make him a helper fit for him.'" And after God had created woman and brought her to Adam, there follow these significant words, "Therefore a man leaves his father and his mother and cleaves to his wife, and they become one flesh" (Gen. 2:18-24). The story of a man and woman whose lives are bound together by love—is the story of mankind.

✣
3. MARRIAGE

At the end of each day of creation as set forth in that
Genesis story God surveyed what he had created and found
that "it was good." On the sixth day, however, there came a
high moment in the drama of creation—God fashioned woman
and presented her to man. It was following this, after joining
man and woman together, the record tells us that "God saw
everything that he had made, and behold, it was *very* good"
(Gen. 1:31). The sense of achievement rose to the superlative
in this final act of creation. Through the ages in perpetuity of
that creation union, man and woman have made the discovery
of an abounding mutual love, have mated under the impulse
of that love, and have "become one flesh"—one life. It was this
that God felt "was *very* good."

The account of Eve created from the rib of Adam was symbolic of the fact that man and woman belong to each other.
"This at last is," said Adam, "bone of my bones and flesh
of my flesh" (Gen. 2:23). Here is revealed the acceptance of
one another as man and woman; two lives that by their love
and desire create the oneness that makes for the complete life
of each person in the marital relation. Marriage, its sanctity, its
importance in man's way of life, carries the profound endorse-
ment of the Scriptures. References to marriage in Genesis
alone are astonishingly real and exact. "Then the Lord God
said, 'It is not good that man should be alone; I will make him

31

a helper fit for him.' " (Gen. 2:18.) "Therefore a man leaves his father and his mother and cleaves to his wife, and they become one flesh." (Gen. 2:24.)

Marriage in the New Testament

This marriage structure was lifted up with added significance by Jesus, who, in answer to the question of the Pharisees concerning divorce, said, "But from the beginning of creation, 'God made them male and female.' 'For this reason a man shall leave his father and mother and be joined to his wife, and the two shall become one.' . . . What therefore God has joined together, let not man put asunder" (Mark 10:6-9).

When you turn to Paul you discover a somewhat different point of view. For a bachelor, Paul had a great deal to say about marriage and the family, and much that he said makes sense. Many of the views of Paul are surprisingly contemporary. It appears that to Paul marriage is the second best way of getting on. His first advice is to remain single. Keep life uncomplicated. He makes it clear that this is his private opinion. "I want you to be free from anxieties." (I Cor. 7:32.) By remaining single you avoid encumbrance. This is best since the time is short, Paul maintained. Here is his real reason for the single life for man: "I think that in view of the impending distress it is well for a person to remain as he is" (I Cor. 7:26). Here Paul sees the end of things as very near, "I mean, brethren, the appointed time has grown very short" (I Cor. 7:29). Actually, according to Paul's preoccupation with the end near at hand, whether you were married or not did not seem to matter too much—"For the whole frame of this world is passing away" (I Cor. 7:31 NEB). While later he changed his view that the end of the world was near, at this particular point he is advising the Corinthians that all would be over soon and therefore they might just as well stay as they were, whether single or married. "Are you bound to a wife? Do not seek to be free. Are you free from a wife? Do not seek marriage." (I Cor. 7:27.) As far as family life is concerned, Paul did not have anything negative to say about it; he had been a guest in too many fine Christian homes.

Paul saw marriage as both exalted and down to earth. "There is neither Jew nor Greek, there is neither slave nor free, there is neither male nor female; for you are all one in Christ Jesus." (Gal. 3:28.) What he means here is that as long as man and woman are one in Christ they are equals. This seems to contradict what the average person knows about the restrictions Paul placed upon woman. Man and woman are equals in the Lord.

ONENESS AND EQUALITY

It is the structure of that oneness of two persons in the marital relation that is the most distinctive, the most implicative, fact of human existence. This same oneness through marriage is embodied in the very origination of life. Here is the validity for the position that the ultimate in human relations is to be found in marriage and the family. It was this union as well as the equality of the sexes that was established in that pristine hour of our human beginning.

For a time this deeper sense of oneness and the equality of

33

the sexes was superseded by the legalism of the early Jewish life of the Old Testament. The inclination was to consider the wife as property. But in spite of this legalism love often prevailed and triumphed over the meniality assigned to womanhood.

When Jesus says, "So they are no longer two but one" (Matt. 19:6), he is affirming monogamy, and more than that, he is affirming marriage as a sacred union not to be broken. Whatever is whole cannot be broken without disaster. Exegetically the words of Jesus make clear that marriage itself is an entity. In the spiritual arithmetic of a conjugal union, one plus one equals one. Two persons through marriage become a third person.

This oneness in marriage provides the basic solidarity of the family. This oneness not only precedes the coming of children into the home, but it lives on after they leave the home. (Increasing longevity means a longer span of years when "Mom" and "Dad" will be together but alone.) Here is the very genius that explains the survival of monogamy.

The writer of Genesis tells us that two persons thus united are on their own; they are to separate from their parents. It is interesting to find back in the origin of things a mandate to in-laws to keep their hands off. "Therefore a man leaves his father and his mother and cleaves to his wife, and they become one flesh." (Gen. 2:24.) Roger Mehl observes, "It is necessary sometimes to insist on the physical sense of this verb to 'leave.' "

One of the most frequent destroyers of marriage solidarity is in-law interference. One woman after marriage would not make the smallest decision without calling her mother on the telephone to request her opinion. As a result the couple did not determine their own affairs. The new home was operated by the not too remote control of the wife's parents. As a last resort, to save the marriage, the young couple was advised to move to another city.

ONENESS WITH DIFFERENCES

There is biblical support for the recognition of differences that can exist within the marriage experience. "Male and female he created them." Differences in the sexes are basic to the marriage fulfillment. Male and female are complementary one to the other. "Too many women," declares Ashley Montagu, "make the mistake of interpreting equal rights to mean that they must become men." Woman is not just the physical opposite of man. Men and women differ as the root and the branch, in characteristics, in perceptions, in reactions. They differ even in the experiences of sexual love. "We are realizing more today than we have for a long time," says William Hulme, "that real suffrage for woman is equality of a woman as being a woman."

We need to realize that to ignore the difference of the sexes would be to ignore the source of much of the richness of the marriage union. Herein is the mystery of the fullness of conjugal life. In the Christian home there can be no value distinction between mother as housewife and father as breadwinner. Each completes the other and thus is created a wholesome and meaningful home. By biblical word man and woman become one as Christ is one with the church. Here is a glorious mystery.

The functions of man and woman within the home are different. The father is the connecting link between home and the life of the world, while the mother provides the constancy of inner warmth and personal care. However, the authority of the home should be expressed by mutual agreement. There is a Spanish proverb that runs, "It goes ill with the house where the hen crows and the rooster is silent." This complementation in marriage is most vital. "Can two walk together," said Amos, "except they be agreed?" (Amos 3:3 KJV.)

Additional Differences

Not only are the differences feminine and masculine, but there are the differences of age, background, tastes, education, and religion. Recently I talked with a boy and girl in their teens determined to marry at once. In addition to being teenagers, the girl is a Roman Catholic, the boy is a Protestant, the girl has only an eighth-grade education, the boy is a junior in college. There were other serious differences which would have to be resolved. How much can the romantic mood in which they are caught up in the present protect these two young people in the midst of the realism of the future if they take this step at this time? Differences can make a tremendous difference in marriage. Divorce rates for those of the same faith is 6.6 percent, for those of different faiths the divorce rate is 15.2 percent. We are told that "persons of widely different faiths or no religious association at all, are five times as likely to end up in the divorce court as those who belong to the same church and who are active in it."

BEHAVIOR DIFFERENCES

There are behavior differences that can cause a marriage to run down like a clock that finally stops ticking. He insists on taking his shoes off in the living room; she persists in talking at him while he tries to read. He goes on hanging trousers from the top drawer of the dresser; she is consistently late for engagements. She continuously makes mistakes in her checkbook arithmetic; he never puts the cap back on the toothpaste tube. Phyllis McGinley says about her own marriage, "He drank coffee to excess and I liked to stay up without it. I was economical, he insouciant about expenses. I forgot to turn out the lights and he put off writing letters. Little things like that." She goes on to say, "And you know what? We reformed each other, we both began to be dilatory together. It was wonderful how friction vanished once we had enough faults in common."

Behaviorist differences can be handled in two ways, either by reform or by reconciliation. In both instances you need to exercise common sense. Someone has said that "a husband is a fellow who expects his wife to be perfect and to understand why he isn't." Husbands and wives who will not reform—and they won't in most cases (he will go on leaving the cap off the toothpaste tube)—let them be reconciled to one another's oddities and errors. In the interest of the deeper experience of unity it would be well for both partners to remember the counsel to "be subject to one another out of reverence for Christ" (Eph. 5:21).

Marriage is not a fifty-fifty matter. It never has been. Marriage is far more a matter of reconciliation, or is it resignation, to each other's foibles and fallacies. Real love is the interpreter always presents the other person to the imagination with favor. Don't lose the interpreter! The husband or the wife, as the case may be, may have to go almost all the way over to the other side. But what of it? This very flexibility is an indication of a wholesome aliveness in the marriage. Of course you can't give in concerning a vitally serious matter to the extent of losing your self-respect. No wife or husband helps the other or helps the marital situation by becoming a mere cipher. At the doorway of the home as the family was leaving, the wife turned to her husband and said, "This time I'm going out and sit in the car and honk the horn while you put on the children's coats."

In all this gamut of differences the marriage can succeed and cohere by a mutual Christian faith. "Whom God had joined together"—God can keep together.

Marriages Can Grow

But marriage will not succeed and grow if it is just a matter of going on. There is more to Christian marriage than just staying married. This is too much like just staying alive. There is nothing very exciting or very complimentary about that. In fact, just staying married is literally a state of marital cold war. Being a party to mere coexistence in a cold war is not Christian.

There are marriages that just wither away. "It's very easy," said Evelyn Waugh in one of his novels, "to not see people at all when you are seeing them all the time." Some marriages vegetate. Some marriages continue by the sufferances of keeping up appearances. Husbands and wives would rather go on being unhappy and remaining together than endure the publicity of a divorce. Such marriages can be ghastly. There is no exchange of confidences, no reaffirmation of deep feeling for each other, no warm, assuring expressions of love, no meaningful sacrifices for each other. This state of "involuntary cooperation," if continued, ends in darkness.

Marriages can grow. They should. Everything that takes place should help that growth. One of the great miracles attached to the Genesis story is growth. Preceding the creation of man, the condition of things was such that no plant, no herb grew in the fields. Then God caused a mist to rise up that watered "the whole face of the ground." It was right then, when the whole earth sprang into life, that God created man. Man began his history to the accompaniment of growth.

The fact is that the health of marriage is both the reason for, and the result of, growth. Successful marriage is evolutional. Sweetness and strength make marriage durable and alive. Growth results from the continued experiences of love's intimacies through the marriage years. It is the ever renewing and reverencing of their meaning for each other that makes the marriage grow.

Equality of Sexes

Let us go back for a moment to the scriptural doctrine of the equality of the sexes. At first glance it looks as though Paul believed in the subordination of woman and the dominance of man, "For man was not made from woman, but woman from man." This is what one author called "chronological priority." "Neither was man created for woman, but woman for man." (I Cor. 11:8, 9.) Paul seems here to regard woman as secondary, but restrain your judgment. Consider the age in which he lived. Paul lived in a man's world. The equality of womanhood as taught by Jesus had to wait centuries for acceptance. But Paul proceeds in verses eleven and twelve to say, "Nevertheless, in the Lord woman is not independent of man nor man of woman; for as woman was made from man, so man is now born of woman. And all things are from God." What an interesting progression in Paul's thinking! Probably with some reluctance, Paul declared man and woman equal in the Lord.

Certainly the domination of the marriage relation by man does not hold the complete support of the point of view of Paul's time. In I Peter we read, "Likewise you husbands, live considerately with your wives, bestowing honor on the woman as the weaker sex, since you are joint heirs of the grace of life" (3:7). The fact is that some women really "ask for it," talking as if being a housewife is negligible business. Being a housewife is no mean vocation. "Every place in the world where men and children come home to sleep or eat or brag of their exploits or plan excursions or be comforted, housewives are concocting that comfort." This is the point of view of Phyllis McGinley. The great experiences of well-being and "of being at home" are made possible by this wonderful vocation.

The basic element in an enduring marriage is respect. Respect in turn rests upon the divine worth of persons established in creation. Here is the place to turn once again to Paul as he says, "Above all these put on love, which binds everything together in perfect harmony" (Col. 3:14). Share everything with one another; money is no problem if there is the right will and strong love. Disharmony is an affliction which comes when people can no longer converse about their marital difficulties. They become judgmental, fearful, and defensive. To be no longer able to communicate in a given marital situation is like a phone call when the other person doesn't hear you, but you are able to hear him. Harmony comes about through love, "a love that never fails," "a love that keeps no score of wrong."

MARRIAGE AND SEX

We come to a consideration of the nature of the sexual aspect of married life as seen in the Scriptures. While Paul himself had little affinity for the Eros experience, he expressed a very sensible and correct view of sex. He knew the risks represented by the great reservoir of emotion. He knew that undisciplined and misdirected it could inundate and destroy a life. But he also knew that in marital life, under the guidance of the spirit of God, this same dynamic could be a source of rare joy, of well-being, and completeness of personal life.

The Christians at Corinth evidently had demanded of Paul to know what a Christian was to do about the sexual life in marriage. "The husband should give to his wife her conjugal rights," Paul said, "and likewise the wife to her husband." Then he continued, "For the wife does not rule over her own body, but the husband does; likewise the husband does not rule over his own body, but the wife does" (I Cor. 7:3, 4). This is the law of sacred mutuality in married life. Paul's expressed understanding was that the sexual life was meant to be creative and hallowed. Let us note two things here, however; first, to be sexually compatible in marriage is no guarantee of either success or happiness. The continuous clash of temperaments can completely eclipse sexual compatibility. It is possible for a couple to be rich or sparing in procreation, yet fail to achieve this wondrous mutuality of which we have been speaking. The important thing is a climate of consummate love in which married people experience these intimacies with their mystery, in keeping with God's will.

Paul goes a step further: "Do not refuse one another," he said, "except perhaps by agreement for a season, . . . but then come together again, lest Satan tempt you through lack of self-control" (I Cor. 7:5). Evidently Paul was talking here about abstinence during the time when conception would be most likely. One could, with some justification, interpret this advice of Paul's as support for the principle of birth control. What realism on Paul's part! Here is the common-sense understanding essential to a successful married life. Here particularly is the scriptural validation of the sexual experience of married people for other than reasons of procreation.

A SPIRITUAL EXPERIENCE

William Hulme calls our attention to the scriptural use of the word "know." "Elkanah knew Hannah his wife, and the Lord remembered her; and in due time Hannah conceived and bore a son, and she called his name Samuel, for she said, 'I have asked him of the Lord.'" (I Sam. 1:19.) "When Joseph woke from sleep, he did as the angel of the Lord commanded him; he took his wife, but knew her not until she had borne a son; and he called his name Jesus." (Matt. 1:24-25.) As Hulme has said, an obviously physical act on the part of man and wife becomes an act of commitment to each other, a renewal of covenant vows, of deep, relating knowing. Biology alone cannot account for this. This is a deep and intimate "knowing," an entering into the deepest mystery together. In "knowing" husband and wife become truly one; in "knowing" there is the all-pervading pride in the possession of each other; in "knowing" there is the sense of having come into the inner court of God's provisioning of wonder and beauty for marital life. It is in this "knowing" that man and woman come nearest to the completeness of each one. Herein is the uniqueness of God's created way.

Obviously the sex experience to be wholly creative must be a spiritual experience. "And whatever you do," Paul says, "in word or deed, do everything in the name of the Lord Jesus, giving thanks to God the Father" (Col. 3:17). Anything short of this is debasement. The significant question concerning sex is not that of participation over against abstention, but rather whether participating or abstaining married persons do so with a resultant growth of love and enrichment of life for both. How else can you resolve the ambiguities of this question? A happy and adequate marriage is a matter of continuous growth in mutual respect and spiritual union.

Paul had an exalted concept of marriage. "Husbands, love your wives, as Christ loved the church and gave himself up for her." (Eph. 5:25.) Man is to love his wife as much as that—like that—and inferentially, a wife is to love her husband that much.

Of course the great experience in Christian marriage is to be found in self-giving. "We love because God first loved us." Out of this kind of love one wills the best for the beloved. Some persons are incapable of giving love because they are incapable of giving themselves. Dag Hammarskjöld once said, "We reach out towards the other. In vain, because we have never cared to give ourselves."

Marriage finds its analogy in discipleship. "He who loses his life for my sake shall find it," is true also of marriage. To fully trust each other, to will the good, the well-being, of the beloved above one's own—herein is the achievement of the highest spiritual level of marriage. As in discipleship, in the true Christian marriage one no longer belongs to one's self. To completely give one's self—this is the great experience in Christian marriage.

An Enduring Marriage

Marriage cannot endure solely on the basis of the physical. This is the hazard in adolescent marriages. On the whole we have oversold physical compatibility and undersold spiritual affinity. In more than one instance, couples well-mated and physically compatible arrive at the brink of divorce. Sexual understanding is needed, but we had better know that it is not a cure-all.

We have more sex information circulating in our society today than ever in our history, but in spite of all this knowledge we note a marked increase in marital breakdown and severance.

THE BIBLE AND DIVORCE

Divorce was permitted in Old Testament times. If a woman found no favor in her husband's eyes because of some reason or other, all he needed to do was to write a bill of divorce, put it in her hand, turn her out, and that was that. (Deut. 24:1-4.) This nettling question of divorce "dogs" us today. Is divorce ever Christian? Jesus maintained that it is not actually a question of legality. Legal dissolubility is possible. Divorce in Old Testament times was obviously unjust to womanhood. This may be the reason for the word, "For I hate divorce, says the Lord the God of Israel" (Mal. 2:16).

Jesus lifted the question up above the "Is it lawful?" level. The simple fact, according to Jesus, is that marriage is permanent. This is his way of revealing the sacredness of womanhood. Jesus was striking a blow at a double standard in regard to marital responsibilities. There were two schools of mind on divorce in Jesus' day: the Shammai position that divorce is allowable only in the instance of adultery; the Hillel school that would allow divorce for other, and sometimes even trivial, reasons. Divorce had long been practiced among the Hebrews. The injustice lay in the fact that only the husband could do the divorcing—and then, often for a slight or petty reason. The law literally meant also that remarriage constituted adultery.

The Pharisees, seeking to put Jesus on the spot and embarrass him in view of the two schools of thought, asked him,

"Is it lawful for a man to divorce his wife?" He answered them, "What did Moses command you?" They said, "Moses allowed a man to write a certificate of divorce, and to put her away." But Jesus said to them, "For your hardness of heart he wrote you this commandment. But from the beginning of creation, 'God made them male and female.' 'For this reason a man shall leave his father and mother and be joined to his wife and the two shall become one.' So they are no longer two but one. What therefore God hath joined together, let not man put asunder" (Mark 10:2-9).

Jesus was saying that divorce was not intended by the Creator. Marriage was meant to be lasting. From the very beginning he appeared to take an absolute position with respect to this. In the original word of Jesus marriage was to be unqualifiedly kept. The spirit of Jesus' word is to be found in the words of our ritual: "Until death us do part."

Paul seemed to leave the door slightly ajar with respect to divorce. In talking about a believing Christian married to an unbelieving person, he said, "But if the unbelieving partner desires to separate, let it be so; in such a case the brother or sister is not bound. For God has called us to peace" (I Cor. 7:15). In the next verse Paul warns against marriage in the face of serious handicap; "Wife," he says, "how do you know whether you will save your husband? Husband, how do you know whether you will save your wife?"

A DAY OF EASY DIVORCE

In a day of easy divorce and still easier remarriage, it may be well to give particular attention to divorce as unthinkable. The Christian position is essentially that to turn one's back on one's marriage is to turn one's back on what is too

priceless to give up. Jesus could not contradict his own pro-
nouncement: "So they are no longer two but one." He went
on to say, "What therefore God hath joined together, let not
man put asunder." The sundering was not to come about because of human meddling or any maneuvering by any man
or woman.

There are places in the Old Testament where this same
judgment of indissolubility is to be found. "And I will betroth
you to me for ever," said Hosea. "I will betroth you to me in
righteousness and in justice, in steadfast love, and in mercy. I
will betroth you to me in faithfulness; and you shall know the
Lord" (Hos. 2:19-20). Helmut Thielicke speaks of this as the
"indelible character of marriage." Paul even goes so far as to
say that in the mixed marriage the union must be maintained.
(I Cor. 7:12-13.) The seriousness with which Paul considers
the matter of a broken marriage covenant is indicated in his
words to the Corinthians, "To the married I give charge, not
I but the Lord, that the wife should not separate from her
husband . . . and that the husband should not divorce his wife"
(I Cor. 7:10).

This principle of spiritual indissolubility becomes the basis
of the conviction that when marriage is under threat, the two
people concerned must exhaust every possibility of not only
making the marriage function, but making it meaningful.
Since marriage is spiritually indissoluble, both parties must
adjust their desires, their notions of personal liberty, to this
abiding and sacred covenant. Ernest van den Haag suggests

in view of some of the common concepts of marrage as temporary
—we would have to reword the marriage vow. Instead of "till

47

death do us part," we might say, "till we get bored with each other." Instead of "forsaking all other"—"till someone better comes along." Clearly if the couple intends to stay married only as long as they want to, they only pretend to be married, they are having an affair with legal trimmings. To marry is to vow fidelity regardless of future feelings.

The marital "drop-out" violates this principle.

We need a new concept of marriage. We need to promote that concept. The Southern Presbyterians in assembly received a report declaring, "As society makes divorce and remarriage more and more easy and socially acceptable, the church must, as did the Apostolic Church in a degenerate pagan society with easy divorce standards quite like our own, insist all the more for her own people on the divine intention of the indissolubility of marriage, save by death." To a Christian the only question is how the marriage covenant is to be conceived. The difference in concept is to be found in the recognition of the eternal nature of marriage. The husband and wife do not start to meet an unpleasant situation with an overwhelming sense of hurt feelings or of denied desires, but with a conviction that life together is God-given and not to be surrendered and not to be injured. The marriage grows stronger every time husband and wife are victors over misunderstanding or dissension. Oddly enough, the same aggravating trouble that drives one couple apart becomes in another instance a reason for a deepening of the unity.

Marriage needs a dynamic. Love must keep expressing itself in the little courtesies that mean so much—the extra phone calls, the note left on the desk, the flower brought on a food tray. Love is more than the fifteen words in a telegram. "Love," someone has said, "is when a fellow takes his hat off in an elevator when he's alone with his wife. Love is something that makes two persons sit close together on a bench even when there is plenty of room." "Love," another person tells us, "makes you buy orchids when you can't afford carnations."

People who find themselves in marital hot water and contemplate throwing marriage overboard little realize how they are going to feel when it happens. Everyone who has tried it knows divorce doesn't solve anything, that it leaves in its wake a wide swath of unhappiness. Children are the real casualties of it. Carefully conducted studies discover that a larger portion of children of divorced or separated persons have lower self-esteem than those whose families are intact. The child faces an adjustment to stepparents on the one hand, or the stress and strain of a situation in which one parent is trying to go it alone. All this is to be understood in the light of what scripturally is so amazingly plain, that is—that in marriage two people become one person.

There are marriages that from the beginning to the end rest on the sacredness of the marriage vow. This word was written by a man more than eighty years of age, who was keeping watch by the bedside of his loved one stricken by illness. The letter, signed in a rather shaky hand, reads in part,

This, my wife's first long illness, tells us how fully we are bound together, that nothing so belongs to us as we belong to each other.

We have a privileged life, especially has mine been such, for it had been with her. We were reared on adjoining farms, went to the country school together, and together attended the State

University. Though she was sought by others, we have always stayed together.

Now in old age, when I most need her, I am at her bedside, privileged to be with her, seeing that her devotion and guidance in the past are an unfailing light at eventide.

✤
4. PARENTS

Responsible parents—this is our prime need. Parental in-
eptitude—this is our current sin. When husbands and wives
become fathers and mothers they face a whole new set of ac-
countabilities. While we are at it, there is the further fact that
you as a parent are in for it, for the duration. Being a parent
is a vacationless job. Whenever discipline is entirely absent,
when parents show no affection, when there is erratic handling
of children, parents are simply asking for trouble.

To develop effective and mature persons in the home, this is
the responsibility of parents. "There is no right way to bring
up a child," Robert Frost wrote to Louis Untermeyer. Perhaps
not, but we can at least avoid some of the wrong ways. One
thing is sure, a child will grow up and become good, bad
or indifferent, depending upon his parents. "You may think it
funny," said a soldier in chance conversation, "but sometimes
I can hear the tick of the kitchen clock at home. It gives me
a wonderful feeling." More than the tick of the clock gave
that soldier a sense of assurance. Something of the indismis-
sable rightness of that home breathed itself out to him. Homes
like that are not too numerous. As one person suggested, the
frightening thing is that parents provide both the heredity and
environment for the growing life. We must grow wholesome
Christian lives, able for a world in which everything goes,
where codes and laws get only casual attention, where people
do not want to get involved.

51

Our obligation to the youth in our homes is made scripturally clear in Paul's word to Titus when he says, "Urge the younger men, similarly, to be temperate in all things, and set them a good example yourself." It would seem that Paul was thinking of us, of our day, when he wrote these words. He goes on to say just how this example is to be set. "In your teaching you must show integrity and high principle, and use wholesome speech to which none can take exception." (Titus 2:6, 7, 8 NEB.)

EXAMPLE

"And set them a good example yourself." Someone said, "If you wish to train up a child in the way he should go, just skirmish ahead on that line yourself." The Revised Standard Version of this same word of Paul reads, "Show yourself in all respects a model of good deeds." Through the medium of our intimacy one with another, in the closeup relation of the home, the kind of living we do has a tremendous effect on those around us, particularly on the young. "Bear down, you are making several copies"—so the instruction reads at the top of the form to be filled out.

Here is where the Christian witness really counts. There is no place where your Christianity is so on trial as in the home, no place where *you* are *you* as in your home. Living one's religion in the home is more important than believing it. The clatter of dishes in the sink is not music; going over the bills on the first of the month is not romance; to face the teacher over at the school where your son is failing is not a happy experience. You have to be a real Christian to keep your buoyancy in the midst of all the realisms of your home life.

Does it make a difference that you are a Christian parent? Does your patience hold out a little longer? Is your expectation of behavior standards a little higher? Are you more sensitive to the spiritual hunger of your child? Are you more aware of each person in the family as of priceless worth? One thing parents need to remember—and it's rather a frightening thing —is, all that goes on in the home goes into the unconscious life of the child. They need to remember also that child behavior is often a matter of imitation—imitation of the adults who people the intimate world of the child.

INTEGRITY

Paul went on to advise Titus, "In your teaching show integrity and high principle"—in your living as well as your teaching. What does parental integrity involve? Children need to experience with their parents, growth, in social concern, in faith in God's provisioning care, in the understanding of right and wrong, in the daily practice of the right and the true.

The integrity of parents does not mean necessarily that they are perfect. It isn't necessary to try to keep up an illusion of perfection. There is nothing wrong with children knowing that their parents are at times in error. In fact there is something wholesome about a parent confessing a mistake. Complete honesty will help provide a solid foundation upon which a child can construct his feeling of confidence about life.

Nor is it a blow to a child's faith to find that a parent has changed his mind about a social view or a religious concept. In fact, it may have just the opposite effect. A parent grows larger in mind and spirit in the eyes of a child when he acknowledges a change in his thinking based on new, or a more complete set of, facts.

The *sine qua non* of integrity is what Paul called "high principle." Parents can make mistakes without injuring a child's trust; they can fail to achieve goals, evidence imperfection in little things—but to relinquish "high principle"— never! A parent can make every material provision for the child's good, spend time with him, be concerned with his school grades, but none of these will make up for showing the white flag of surrender in the matter of principle. "We spend so much time," one man commented, "planning to give our children things we didn't have that we forget to see that they have, at least, some of the things we did have."

ADULT FAILURE

Paul had much to say about what constitutes Christian conduct. He would have more reason to say it today. "Let all your behaviour be such as even pagans can recognize as good, . . . they will come to see for themselves that you live good lives, and will give glory to God." (I Peter 2:12 NEB.) Later in the same epistle he wrote, "For it is the will of God that by your good conduct you should put ignorance and stupidity to silence" (2:15 NEB). This is good advice to parents.

ADULT BEHAVIOR

The parental vocation of moral discipline has been in decline. The fact is that our adult world is in bad shape morally. If there is something wrong with our children, it may be because there is something wrong with us as adults. We can shake our heads and wring our hands about the youngsters of today, but we are not right ourselves. In a recent poll of 845 teenagers taken by the Luther League of America, 87 percent of these youngsters admitted that they cheat. The editor of the League's magazine says of adults, "Stories of embezzlement, glorification of expense accounts and polite and courteous cheating in business and social worlds are only indications that we ourselves are filled with the problem. We've only graduated to more professional cheating." This adult wrongdoing has its influence on the young mind. As one young person in a home said, "How do you keep up to the standards you believe in, how do you keep from getting corrupted, when nobody is around to symbolize the higher things?" Our moral fabric has been weakened by under-the-table dealing, hidden charges, the resort to legal loopholes. It is what Margaret Halsey calls "the mongrelization of our ethics." Our collective looseness is a betrayal of the growing child.

As adults we have accepted wrongdoing by consensus. The most disturbing fact connected with cheating in the classroom is the attitude of parents. Teachers find parents defending the child's dishonesty—"He has to make good grades to get into college." "Other children do it." "It's only that my boy got caught." These parents were making amply evident why their children cheat. Harry Emerson Fosdick once said, "In the past day the question was, how can we have tolerance when we must live up to our convictions? Today the question is, how can we have convictions when we must be true to our tolerance?" Cheating and lying are gaining more approval every day. There is a growing moral permissiveness in which sexual deviation and ethical deterioration vie with each other for our common acceptance. We need to remind ourselves that we become a part of what we tolerate! We have descended from the level of being soft about evil to being sentimental about what is downright vile and filthy. A novel, a play, or a picture can be filthy, but if the characters in it are honest about their filth all seems to be well. What a descent!

Where is the church in all of this? People expect guidance as to what is Christian in a badly mixed-up culture. Christianity must restore our moral and ethical absolutes.

We are greatly exercised about corruption in high places, but we need to be more concerned with corruption in ourselves. Children need to learn the truth about life, not from T.V. and not from indulgence in the big time or the push for prestige, but from the moral idealism of sound parents and the disciplined life of an upright home. A child has a right to a heritage of moral fitness.

Home is still the place where good character and sound values of life are to be passed on to the next generation—

> things that we have heard and known,
>   that our fathers have told us.
> We will not hide them from their children,
>   but tell to the coming generation
> the glorious deeds of the Lord, and his might,
>   and the wonders which he has wrought.

>   . . . .

> That the next generation might know them,
>   the children yet unborn,

and arise and tell them to their children,
    so that they should set their hope in God,
and not forget the works of God,
    but keep his commandments (Ps. 78:3-7).

PARENTAL HARMONY

Paul advises, "And above all these put on love, which binds everything together in perfect harmony" (Col. 3:14). Certainly the integrity of parents includes marital agreement of mind—deeper still, marital harmony. Growth within the family, the development of a religious life, and the well-being of each member, dictate the necessity of parental accord that has its roots in a lasting marital unity. From this comes a continuing climate of good feeling within the home. Studies made by P.T.A.'s show a marked correlation between child failure in school and the marital unhappiness of parents.

The oneness of parents should extend to an agreement concerning the nurture and the discipline of children. In one investigation where wives were interrogated about disagreement with their husbands, it was reported that the greatest degree of disagreement, 26 percent, concerned itself with child rearing and discipline. You can put it down as a fairly consistent rule that when parents do not get along with each other, they do not get along with their children.

STABILITY

Responsible parenthood and parental integrity add up to a stability in home life—a stability that engenders respect for persons, for property, for the rules of the game. Paul wrote to the Colossians, "As for you children, your duty is to obey your parents, for at your age this is one of the best things you can do to show your love for God" (3:20 Phillips). This advice of Paul to children is a kind of New Testament fifth commandment. Phyllis McGinley startles the reader with the following,

The longer I lived in a house with children, the less importance I put on cooperatively threshing out matters of conduct or explaining to them our theories of discipline. If I had to do it over again, I wouldn't reason with them at all until they arrived at an age of reason—approximately 21. I would give them rules to follow, I would try to be just, and I would try even harder to be strict. I would do no arguing. Children in their hearts like laws. Authority implies an ordered world, which is what they—and in the long run, most of the human race—yearn to inhabit. In law there is freedom. Be too permissive and they feel lost and alone.

Someone needs to create a film entitled "The Wonderful World of the Home"—a medium to make explicit the presence and the usefulness of order and its consequent authority. Authority should not dictatorially be exercised, but inferred from reasonableness and common sense on the part of the parent. Instead of arbitrary judgments, condemnation without hearing, why not let the truth of the situation do the judging? The guidelines by which the whole family is to live can be constructed in such a way that fairness obtains in every situation. Give up this structure or rules in the name of total liberty, and you end up with juvenile anarchy. "Fifty years ago," someone said, "minding one's children did not mean obeying them."

Order does not mean blind conformity. Absolute conformity never produced a creative spirit in anyone. On the other hand, order in the home does not mean an unchanging green light, indicating that everything goes. It isn't easy for a home to achieve a sensible balance between order and freedom. It is not a question of authority and obedience being old or new. The simple fact is that you cannot have stability or growth without them. Without order within the home children do not grow. The strain particularly during adolescent years, the awkwardness of coping with those demands that come with the first dawn of adulthood, make very necessary for the adolescent a stable, dependable home.

There are some qualifications to be attached to the parental exercise of authority. There must be understanding and consistency in the behavior attitudes of parents. There must be in parental attitudes a basis for a youngster's trust. Authority, no matter how it is exercised, may be greatly hindered by a lack of candor, by a possessiveness, and by a total imposition of adult thinking without any attempt to share.

Children really want order and expect rules. Seventy-five percent of one group of teenagers stated that "obedience and respect for authority are the most important habits for children to learn." The Gilbert Youth Research Company, an organization conducting regular surveys on teenagers' views, disclosed that more than half of 4,591 youngsters questioned in a coast-to-coast check felt that teenage delinquents are not being handled sternly enough. More than fifty percent of them felt that their parents, schools, churches, and law-enforcement agencies coddled them too much. The Christian home is one that believes in order—believes that mother and father have special functions that, when put together, make for thoughtful and just control.

Family life may not be a peaceful dream, but it certainly need not be a demoralizing disarray. Where there is genuine love between parents, where harmony has gained some domestic history, where understanding is more important to a parent than egotistical satisfaction, where generosity concerning other members of the family is healthily exercised, where neither parent is haunted by a disordering sense of guilt—you have a basis for a kind of family life, propitious, auguring well for all its future.

✤

5. FAMILY

From the beginning, human life has been found to exist in families. A family form has continued through the ages. It may be in a trailer court or a fishing boat, it may be rural or urban, it may be in a high-rise apartment or a single room—if a family lives there it is a place of infinite importance. It's a place where man and wife, father and mother and children, dream, pray, plan, and grow up together. It's a place where loved ones know the joy of birth and the sorrow of death. It's a place that houses the most vital institution on earth—a family. Everyone begins life as a person but also as a member of a family. Roger Mehl says, "It is through the medium of a family, not as a detached individual, that a person is rooted in humanity."

At the base of everything is the family. That's why the subject of a family never grows stale. The family is where the soul grows tall and where the real meaning of life is found and possessed. Little wonder then that William E. Hocking would observe, "It is perhaps not too much to say that the Christian family comes close to being an absolute for Christianity, a necessary consequence of its own universal precept. It is a natural context for a sacrament inasmuch as it is by way of human love that the divine is most frequently and completely discovered."

THE FAMILY AND HISTORY

The institution of the family is as old as humanity. In the light of recent findings our social scientists have concluded that our earliest ancestors, known as cave men, established family relationships akin to those of our day. They did not lead the disorganized way of life generally attributed to them. As one author stated, "Their partnership duration would put Hollywood to shame." The roles of father and mother are ancient roles, founded largely upon the necessity of caring for and nurturing the young. The archaeologist, James Breasted, once said, "It is obvious that the long dependence of helpless little children on the support and protection of father and mother had much to do with softening and refining the early savagery of man and transforming it into solicitude and affectionate concern for the welfare of wife and children."

The family did not just happen. God began the family—"male and female he created them." The family began with creation. The whole earth was brought forth by the Creator, and then God said to man, "Here is a whole world of growing, living things for your use." You know the rest of the story.

THE OLD TESTAMENT AND THE FAMILY

Two thousand years ago—yes, three thousand years ago—families were much as they are now. Change the scene a bit—sons were cherished as of more value than daughters, fathers were more completely in charge, the control of the home was more legalistic; however, the characteristics of loyalty, a sense of solidarity, pride, honor, and respect were known then as well as now.

There is no getting around it, the father figure of the Old Testament day was the primary force in the home. In spite of the patriarchal system of his day, however, the father was not always savagely harsh. The scriptural word "like as a father pitieth his children" indicates a good measure of paternal compassion. Contrary to what you may expect, mother was mighty important in her own way. She had considerable authority. Sarah told Abraham to put Hagar out of the house—and he did. Mother possessed other qualities. The prophet speaks of the ability of mother to comfort her family (Isa. 66: 13). Note the feeling that Joseph, as a son, had for his father, Jacob—a feeling at times overshadowed by a healthy egotism on his part. He delayed the reunion with his family while enjoying the exercise of his authority in faraway Egypt, nevertheless Joseph's love for his father and the nostalgic longing for his home folks is unmistakable.

The profusion of references to these fundamental marital and family relations in the Old Testament is nothing short of amazing.

THE FAMILY IN NEW TESTAMENT TIMES

The importance of the family to scriptural writers of the New Testament is seen in the elaborate genealogies setting forth the ancestry of Jesus. Matthew's Gospel states that Jesus was the son of David, the son of Abraham (1:1 KJV). Luke goes a step further and traces the ancestry of Jesus all the way back to Adam. (Luke 3:23-38.) The Christian family began in Bethlehem—"for to you is born this day in the city of David a Savior, who is Christ the Lord" (Luke 2:11).

The Christian family and its activity and relationships began a new tradition in the pagan world. There came into being a design of life, customs, and practices that marked the Christian family with certain distinctions. The Christian family was different in its way of life, its ethical standards, its regard for others, the respect which members of the family held for one another, and its faith in God.

In its rich and creative interdependence of one member upon the other, the Christian family finds its validity in the Scriptures. In his letter to Titus, Paul says,

Bid the older men be temperate, serious, sensible, sound in faith, in love, and in steadfastness. Bid the older women likewise to be reverent in behavior. . . . They are to teach what is good, and so train the young women to love their husbands and children, to be sensible, chaste, domestic, kind, and submissive to their husbands, that the word of God may not be discredited. Likewise urge the younger men to control themselves. Show yourself in all respects a model of good deeds, and in your teachings show integrity (2:2-7).

It was this interaction within the home, young and old, men and women, the effect of one member upon the other in the spirit of Christ, that had much to do with the tremendous impact of Christianity upon the society and culture of the Roman world. Here is an astonishing blueprint of family conduct for grandparents, wives, husbands, and youth—rules of the game of living together that one observes make for a happy, wholesome home. This view of a family, of older persons, husbands, wives, parents, and children—a coherent whole—is a picture of family life in its uniqueness.

What is a family? A family consists of individuals plus something else—the collective mind, feeling, and will of its members. The family is the unity of persons, developing and fulfilling their lives through the interaction of love of one upon the other.

What is the function of a family? The family needs to know its business and mind it; a family provides an intimacy that meets the desire for meaningful companionship and satisfies that universal desire of the individual to belong; it provides a relationship with adults that helps the growing life develop an effective self-image and gives guidance for the proper and responsible relation of that growing person to God and his world.

TRUSTEESHIP OF THE FAMILY

One thing apparent in Paul's letter to Titus is that attitudes, traditions, and values vital to a sound way of life are to be passed on through the trusteeship of the family. Older women were to teach young women to love their husbands, to be models of right living, to teach what is good. Actually Paul is describing the family as a school of life.

Older people are to "be sensible" in the homes of their children. They are not only to be "sound in faith" but in charity and in patience. Could it be that Paul is telling grandparents that they ought to be understanding and patient in respect to the way their sons and daughters run their homes? It is hard for grandparents to refrain from taking over the wheel when they come to visit or stay in the homes of their sons and daughters.

The Apostle even reminds the members of the family that they ought to be "sound in speech in the home." Don't fling words around like the indiscriminate use of a garden hose. Don't talk in the cheap jargon of the street. Fathers, don't continuously talk shop. Mothers, beware of persistent nagging. Let the conversation of the home be sometimes jocular, sometimes serious, but always wholesome. The words of loving inquiry, of careful admonition, of assurance, forgiveness, and of witness that goes with real believing—these are the servants of the kind of speech that should be heard in the home. Further, parents, listen to your children. The common complaint of children is that adults will not listen.

Paul turns to the younger men to say to them that as husbands and fathers, "show yourselves as models of good deeds in teaching, show integrity." Where is Christianity to be lived more than in the home? What a place of Christian witness! "Children need models more than they need critics."

These are some of the responsibilities that when met make for a proper climate for the exercise of trusteeship. Members of a family are the trustees of its blood, its right, its name. Here is tremendous power and equally tremendous privilege. The example of spiritual and moral values, the teaching of the lessons of community, the conditioning to Christian attitudes —these are the means whereby the Christian family passes on to the new generations its way of life and thus faces accountably its trusteeship.

The family will survive not only because of its agelong history, but it will survive also because of its indispensability as trustee of moral and social values.

THE HOME WITH NOTHING IN IT

The image of the family is born in the soul. The home inlays the very soul of man. William Saroyan tells of the soldier coming home from the Korean war to Ithaca, California. Limping a bit, this soldier walked slowly about, looking at everything, talking to himself. "This is Ithaca," he said. "There is the depot—the Santa Fe, and there is the Ithaca sky over it. This is the public library, there is the Presbyterian Church, there is the Ithaca High School, this is the athletic field and there's Santa Clara Avenue and Ara's Market. There is the House! There it is. There's my home!" Here was the climax of all of his longing. You will never erase the image of a family out of the mind of man. In spite of the fact that the home as we idealize and idolize it is embedded in our very beings, the actual thing itself can be a tawdry semblance of that image in our hearts.

The great question of our times is what shall the home exist for. The spiritual graces of family living have been crowded out of the heart of the home by the plausible illusion of material things. These quiet strengths, and the deep inner feeling of well-being that they give the home, are being offered upon the altar of things.

The author of the first Epistle of Peter has a word to say to wives. "Your beauty should reside, not in outward adornment—the braiding of the hair, or jewelry, or dress—but in the inmost centre of your being, with its imperishable ornament, a gentle, quiet spirit, which is of high value in the sight of God." (3:3-4 NEB.) Further in verse 7 he gives his reason for this advice, "because you [husband and wife] share together in the grace of God which gives you life." This preoccupation with "adornment" that he talks about has infiltrated the entire life of the home.

One after the other of our homes goes in for adornment and loses the grace of God by which the home receives its life. Fifty years ago the beginning home faced 119 wants of which 17 were absolute necessities. Today the beginning home faces 973 wants of which 117 are absolute necessities. "The world is so full of a number of things, I am sure we should all be as happy as kings"—but we are not! Affluence can curse as well as bless.

The family is suffering from the coarsening influence of mass media, the growing absenteeism of fathers who are home on weekends only, the increasing employment of mothers (by 1970 more than 4 out of every 10 women will be holding paying jobs), but most of all the immersion in things.

Christianity had better go to work on the conscience of the home. We need a new kind of temperance, a temperance about things—"adornments," appliances, gadgets, furnishings—and a restoration of mindfulness of the grace of God without which homes cannot exist. We think, act, and live as though well-being is a matter of "living electrically," or a well-stocked freezer. Recently there have been advertised an electric card shuffler and a pair of cuff links which will give you the temperature centigrade and Fahrenheit. What does the home exist for? Isn't it true that a home has a mission in the same sense that a person has a mission? What are you doing about your home beside furnishing it and keeping it going?

The great struggle of our contemporary time is for the soul of the home. The stark consequence of the secularism of our day is the empty home—the kind of home that has nothing to live up to and nothing to hand down. "We let our young people down when we let them think our high standards of living are an end in themselves rather than a means to an end," said Nelson Bell. To people of the empty home the need for God seems utterly irrelevant. To them religion is vestigial, functionless, inapplicable. Secularism deadens the moral and spiritual sensitivity. What has being a Christian got to do with a Mediterranean cruise, an FHA loan, a new hairdo, a hi-fi set, or, for that matter, a cure for mental illness or the cold war?

When you say "my home" you mean something abiding, something of the sacred because God is in it. Forget the adornments, we read in I Peter, be sure that you have the "imperishable ornaments," the quiet spirit, and most of all the shared "grace of God" in your home.

FAMILY LIMITATION

Any discussion about the family will lead sooner or later to a discussion of family limitation. The limitation of the number of children in the family is, in many parts of the world, the most pressing question of our day.

In America, at least for the time being, the question is solving itself. However, the lull in the number of births in America is likely to prove temporary. While a decade ago larger families were in evidence, young couples today are having fewer children. The birth rate for every 1,000 women has dropped from 123 in 1957 to 98 for the year 1965. Nobody seems to be sure of the reason. Some couples mention the rising cost of living, others speak of the mounting cost of a college education, and then there is the argument of the trend toward economy-sized homes. It may be just a matter of fashion to have a smaller family today, and fashions change. For the present at least, the trend in America is toward the smaller family.

GROWTH OF POPULATION

The astounding growth of population the world over makes the question of the exercise of choice regarding the birth of persons in a given family a crucial one. What shall Christian parents do? Theology may have something to say about this question. There are people who feel that limiting birth is tampering with God's law and will. Certainly great care needs to be exercised in respect to persons who may experience a sense of guilt in limiting birth, more particularly concerning the use of the means of birth limitation. Serious consideration is essential so as not to precipitate guilt feelings, which in turn may affect emotional stability and health. As one writer put it, "The Christian's belief regarding the use of contraceptives must be related to the meaning and purpose of marriage as determined by a study of the Scriptures."

One of the questions we meet at this point is whether or not sexual relations exist, under the providence of God, not alone to bring children into the world but for the enrichment and deepening of the mystic forces of marital life.

But regard further this population dilemma. During the approximate time it would take to read this chapter the world population will have increased by 4,200 persons. By the end of the twentieth century the population of the world will in all likelihood reach the seven billion mark, and by the end of the twenty-first century—think of it—the population will have reached the staggering standing-room-only figure of 100 billion—unless we accomplish worldwide appreciable family limitation.

Any question of birth limitation is fundamentally a spiritual matter—a matter of responsible cocreationship with God.

There are persons who say that the claims for birth control are not clear. They point to the command in Genesis to "be fruitful and multiply" (1:28). There seems to be no ambiguity here, at least not sufficient to provide cover for a plea for birth control. We do have the right, however, to insist that this command be seen in the light of today's circumstances. In part importance lies in the difference between a naturalistic world and a highly mechanistic world. Certainly it is true also that we cannot interpret this command aside from the true meaning of that mystical and intimate relation of men and women essential to fruitfulness. Further, there is not a little difference between the Genesis day and our own. In that early time what would point to happiness or the crowning of human life more than the divine directive to "be fruitful and multiply"?

We must realize that this command, "be fruitful and multiply," was given in the setting of a creative narrative in which the earth itself was so plentiful that it could support a plentiful population. This is not true today. Further, this command was met out of a naïveté of life—which in view of demographic disclosures we can no longer sustain—a naïveté that today would approach a condition of irresponsibility. Certainly the birth of a human being incidental to a sexual experience with no thought of the future of this new life or its possibilities of achieving fulfillment, cannot be considered a matter of divine will. There is a limit to which one can elevate naïveté toward the level of infinity.

There are those who would declare that the Genesis command would imply that any restriction of birth is not of God —is not of his natural law. On the other hand, the law of God's grace mediated for us in the interest of the fullness of life for all human beings constitutes one of God's higher laws. Parents under the guidance of the Holy Spirit will decide to limit or not to limit fertility according to the conditions that will make for the glory of God in the whole earth.

In addition to what has been said here, this decision to limit or not to limit birth must be seen in terms of social responsibility—in the light of what Thielicke speaks of as "the moral necessity" of our time. The question is really one of biological processes seen in terms of Christian ideals concerning the well-being of persons. There is an element of otherness in this question that, given our Christian principles, is inescapable. What is greatly essential is to establish right motives. Not only must consideration be given to the consequences of unlimited birth in terms of deprivation within a given family, but also in terms of the serious injury to the welfare of the larger community as well. The family of man must see its responsibility to the communities of the world. The Christian family and demographical implications are in direct relationship here. Jesus demonstrated this larger view when he asked, "Who is my mother and who are my brothers?" Certainly the well-being that God intended for all human life cannot be achieved aside from the full life of each person.

We believe that the conquest of disease and the subsequent increase of longevity are of God. But we also believe that the right of any person born into the world to human dignity and the fullness of life are of God. The real hope of the future lies with responsible parenthood.

THE RELEVANCE OF THE CHRISTIAN WAY

There is a singular relevance about Christ in the home. The discharge of parental responsibility in such a way as to obtain a happy, wholesome home life comes about when Christ is the companion of family life. Carle Zimmerman in his volume on the family said, "Familism is a system that must be built largely from within." The Christian family is that historic form of life in which the best relations can be obtained when the members of it are Christian.

There is no more appropriate biblical word to present at this point than that of Paul to the Colossians, when he says, "And whatever you do, in word or deed, do everything in the name of the Lord Jesus, giving thanks to God the Father" (3:17). John Henry Jowett once prayed, "O Lord, keep me sensitive to the grace that is around about me. May the familiar not become neglected. May I see thy goodness in my daily bread, and may the comfort of my home take my thoughts to the mercy seat of God!"

♣
6. MOTHERS AND FATHERS

It is often said of the widow left with small children, "And now she must be a father to them, too." It is fair to infer that the performances of father and mother are two different things. There is some confusion at this point. Motherhood and fatherhood do not exist in separate compartments. Both mother and father give affection and provide security and well-being; both are concerned about the child's comfort, discipline, and growth. But by the very nature of their roles in the family's life father and mother have specialties in functions.

The mother, by reason of being a mother, is in closer contact with a child from its birth. For example, the problems of a boy of five years evolve in a daily world where mother is the one to whom to turn. Given a few years, however, there is a change; the boy begins to identify with his father increasingly and to transfer to him the daily needs for counsel and encouragement. There is a difference in handling a tiny child. A mother is gentle and holds a child tenderly; a father plays rather roughly but with a kind of certainty that makes the child unafraid and even feel secure.

In the main a mother relates the child to the inner world of intimate things, the father to the outside world of life and events. A mother, because of her close-up relation, schools the child in necessary regimen, habits, and practices that have to do with good behavior, with the virtues of unselfishness, forgiveness, fair play. The father orients the child to a life of work, a world of sports, of public morality, the things that have to do with extras and character.

MOTHERS

Mother's role in the home has been unduly conceived of as commonplace. Henry Bowman observed:

If a woman teaches someone else's children, she is accorded professional status; if she teaches her own children, she is "just a mother." If she studies dietetics and has charge of a large kitchen in a restaurant or institution, she has a profession; but if she applies dietetic facts and principles to the feeding of her husband and children, she is just cooking.

One woman who was chosen by her community for special honor as a mother responded, "Who me? I've never done anything. I just brought up a houseful of kids to be decent women and men, that's all." Women whose main responsibility is the home are self-consciously inclined to downgrade homemaking. Harry Peelor tells of a truck driver in a quiz show interrupting his wife who in answer to the question said that she was a housewife. "You are not," he objected, "you are my wife." Mrs. Billy Graham feels that "to believe that homemaking is a divinely appointed task is not to take the spice out of living. I am not here by accident. I am where God put me, doing the task for which He created me. My task is second in importance to none, including preaching."

To love a home, to live in it, to work in it and for it, is

scripturally recommended. Paul in his letter to Titus urged younger women (young mothers) to love their husbands and children—"to be sensible and chaste, home lovers" (2:4, 5 Phillips). The New English Bible translates this last phrase "busy at home." How can she help it! A survey in London revealed that housework takes forty hours a week; a child under two occupies an extra ten hours; and an infant under one an additional twenty hours. The same survey proved that a woman with all the automation she can lay her hands on still walks one third of the way around the world as she accomplishes twenty years of household chores.

What about mothers who are employed? Many words appear in print or are spoken from the platform concerning this question of mothers employed outside the home. The question is, can a mother do a good job of it in the home and yet be gainfully employed? This question obviously must take into consideration such factors as the age of the child or children involved, the necessities leading to employment, the provision made for the care of children after school.

Being a mother is a full-time job. Anyone can easily argue that it is essential that mother be around all day. If a mother is going to be aware of the feelings of the child, the happenings that affect it for good or ill, she will have to be on the scene. You can't save up the little crises or disasters that children encounter during the day and schedule them for treatment at a convenient time.

We are tackling a life-sized issue here. A study made by the Chase Manhattan Bank reveals that one out of every five workers is a married woman. According to the Department of Health, Education, and Welfare, two out of five working women are mothers of children of school age. Four hundred thousand children under twelve years of age must care for themselves while their mothers work.

But there are two sides to the question. Dr. Alberta Sigel, of Pennsylvania State University, asserts that working mothers are here to stay. One of the Assistant Secretaries of Labor, speaking of women working, intimates that this is all to the good. "They have made it possible for millions of families to attain higher standards of health and to provide more education for their children, as well as to buy more homes, household appliances and cars."

As far as their marital life is concerned, the wives who are "moonlighting" seem to get on equally well with their husbands. Authorities tell us that the real problems develop with mothers who are off and on as workers outside the home— the mothers who "flit erratically from job to job." However, a mother who is unstable emotionally may affect her children adversely though she is not occupied outside the home.

One could justly go on to say that a mother needs to have concerns beyond the home other than those that would involve her in gainful employment. She needs to broaden her point of view, to refresh her mind and reestablish her sense of self-worth by meaningful relations within the community. Occupation with the affairs of a community seems to be validated by the Scriptures. The writer of Proverbs describing an exemplary wife says, "She opens her hand to the poor, and reaches out her hands to the needy." This writer goes on to say, "She makes linen garments and sells them" (31:20, 24).

Of course, it's a question of the character of the interest that the mother is concerned with in the community. A social columnist in one of our daily papers reports, "Young matrons meeting for the conservation and preservation of African violets." It is quite hard to justify some of our community time-consuming activities. There are women who are habitual "downtowners." They know every counter and every sales-person in every store.

Much of the emigration of mothers from the home is for other than gainful employment. Some mothers involved so constantly in community and social activities are away from home as much as if they were employed. The exodus from the home is encouraged by the use of such devices as electric dishwashers that work while you are on your way.

Regardless of their outside responsibilities or interests, the greatest essential for mothers is to remain "home lovers," "busy at home," sensitive to the needs of their loved ones, pro-viding from warm hearts the answer to the hunger to belong and helping restore courage and strength of faith. "Busy at home," or busy in the community, mother must develop a contemplative mind, granting out of her closeness to God a largess of spiritual good and light to her family. When she is at her best, she guides with incredible understanding the groping heart, sees deep into the inner turmoil, intuitively grasps the reason for distress, and, because of her quiet faith, is able to help the troubled one know peace. This is the gift and genius of motherhood.

FATHERS

Father by nature and providence is best adapted to inter-pret social responsibilities and the affairs of public life, as well as world situations, to the growing mind, to aid in the orientation of the child to an ever-widening environment, to help him become a good citizen, and to guide him in the choice of his vocation. In addition, of course, the father is a companion on fishing expeditions, at ball games, or in the activity of some hobby.

Some children were asked for their ideas of a father's duties. Here are some of the replies. "Daddies are to build boats and spank children." "Fathers are to go to work." "Fathers are to take care of children when mothers have to go some place." These definitions were very revealing of individual home situations. Fathers seem to have a rather heavy assignment. One little tot prayed, "God bless mother, God bless baby brother, God help daddy."

Father epitomizes the authority of whatever order the home has established. In the past the father was a bread-winner; he was to earn the money, and mother was to raise the children. There is more of a partnership in today's home, particularly in the home where the mother is employed. This partnership situation has gained momentum from the growing instances of early marriage and the mounting incidence of the wife working to help the husband through college. Someone said that today there are more women working outside the home and more men on the inside.

Much of this is good. However, there is some current opinion to the effect that father is growing too domestic, that his distinctly fatherly influences are being submerged in domesticity, that he is becoming a kind of assistant manager of the home. Homes can be found where the situation is just the opposite. There are the absentee fathers—the weekend fathers, who journey out on Sunday night and return to their homes on Friday evening. William Hulme thinks that "we have gone from too much man in the home to no man." It is a little difficult for a father to dispense enough affection and manifest enough concern for his children in two days to last through the week.

In all of this the important thing is the father's stance. How to exercise authority, to counsel youngsters in the midst of their growing-pains problems—this calls for real art as well as genuine understanding. If father is to be in control, it means that he must handle the job with grace as well as strength. The Gluecks of Harvard claim that "the most effective guard against delinquency is a father who is at the same time both strict and loving."

In writing to the Ephesians Paul said, "You fathers, again, must not goad your children to resentment, but give them the instruction, and the correction, which belong to a Christian upbringing" (6:4 NEB). To be restrained, to be firm, to discipline without anger, to admonish without making a child feel inferior require both self-control and patience. We are at an important point here. Father arrives at the time fatigued with the day's work with a high potential for irritation. It is also true that the children may be just as nervously depleted after a whole day of school and play. Father must be able to listen to their recitals of experiences and their questions—they will all try to talk at once. To listen, to make real inquiry, to note the rivalry for his attention, to laugh with the children—the father enters into all this with wholesome and genuine interest.

The family, of course, is a joint enterprise in which every

member should feel free to contribute his or her opinion. Father performs like an orchestra leader, assimilating and interpreting all that is contributed in terms of what is best for all. His should be a tempered and reasonable exercise of authority. Paul saw the point of this. "Fathers, don't overcorrect your children or make it difficult for them to obey the commandment." (Eph. 6:4 Phillips.)

Perhaps the most valid criticism of fathers is that they are not deeply nor consistently aware enough, not seeing the profundity of their part in the family drama. Some fathers think they've done the best they can when they provide a home and sacrifice to make possible a good education for their children. But the responsibility of fatherhood is a matter of deeper empathy, of entering into the deeper emotional experiences of his children with understanding. Paul exhorted the Ephesian fathers to "bring them [children] up with Christian teaching in Christian discipline." The price is high. This means more than being a pal to your child. One commentator said, "I have a dark suspicion that if there were more parents and fewer buddies in America's families, many children would be a good deal more mannerly and a whole lot less spoiled. Not only that, they would grow up to be finer, more confident, more secure adults." You can be close to your boy or girl without becoming a "school chum" to them. As one person put it, "The kids don't need a middle-aged pal."

Further, it is not a question of the amount of time you spend with your child. The important thing is to be with him every moment you are together, consciously and wholeheartedly. This identity of father and child in order to be wholesome and helpful must be an unself-conscious one. One of the great needs is that the father's own experience of God be felt in the companionship with the child. This is what makes for a sense of timeless purpose imparted by him to his family.

GOD THE FATHER

Whether you wish it or not as a father, your child thinks of God favorably, resentfully, or indifferently, depending on how he feels about you as his father. It was said of Martin Luther, according to William Barclay in his book *The Mind of Jesus,* that "he hesitated to pray the Lord's Prayer and to say 'Our Father' because his own father had been so strong, so unbending, so unsympathetic, that the word father was not a word which he loved." When a boy's relation to his father is close, satisfying, confidence-growing, he will feel whole-hearted in his praying, "Our Father who art in heaven." To believe in God's constancy may necessitate more constancy evidenced in the life of his father.

Louis Linn and Leo W. Schwarz, in writing about the religious life of small children, tell us,

This period is characterized initially by a conception of God which differs little from the child's conception of his own parents. At this phase of development, the child commonly pictures God as possessing the attributes of his father, or occasionally his mother. He may say that God is like his father only larger. Gordon W. Allport cites the case of a six-year-old boy who refused to recite the "Our Father" prayer because his earthly father was a drunkard. The opposite reaction is exemplified by a girl of five who was excessively attentive to her father both in public and in private. He filled all her thoughts and made her happy and wholly over-shadowed even her religious life. When at prayer, she felt far more religious fervor if she was looking at her father as she prayed.

It is natural for a child to look up to his father. No father is quite the hero that his daughter thinks he is nor quite the man his son thinks he is, but if he loves his children so much that they know it, they will find little difficulty in coming to the Heavenly Father in full trust. In tribute to his father, Thomas Carlyle once wrote, "On the whole, ought I not to rejoice that God was pleased to give me such a father; that from the earliest years I had the example of a real man of God's own making continually before me? Let me learn of him. Let me write my book as he built his houses, and walk as blamelessly through this shadow world."

THE RELIGIOUS LIFE OF THE HOME

Mothers and fathers are jointly responsible for the religious life of the home. There is no automation that can be sub-stituted for conscious, intelligent, parental accompaniment in the spiritual venture of children.

In a general way your children may be getting a smattering of this or that in religion. The spiritual life of the child must grow as he grows. How important is God in the living that goes on in your home? You may agree that religion is a good thing, but that is not enough to grow the religious life of your children. Fathers and mothers will have to be spiritual persons—persons of daily experiences with God.

✤
7. CHILDREN

"Children, obey your parents in everything, for that is pleasing to God and is the Christian way. Fathers, do not exasperate your children for fear they grow disheartened." (Col. 3:20-21 NEB.)

In asking children to obey their parents Paul is making reference to the fifth commandment. If you believe that this commandment was divinely inspired, then you believe that children should be subject to the direction of their parents. In exhorting children to be obedient Paul makes guidance, and discipline as well, undebatable. However, conditions have changed so vastly over the centuries we are obligated to examine the meaning of Paul's words for our own times.

In spite of the centuries which have intervened, Paul is most contemporary in his point of view. In Colossians he is cautioning fathers to be temperate and reasonable in the exercise of their discipline. When you come to the modern situation, what should a parent do? Many parents are in despair. Nothing seems to work. Part of the trouble seems to lie in both the form and practice of control as influenced by the temperament of the parent. Some objective thinking would help. "What will work best in view of the kind of a boy he is?" Too little or too much control are common parental sins. The mother who declared that her theory of child rearing was "carefully supervised neglect" may be saying something to us very worthwhile. One mother prayed, "Let me not be too ready to guide my children's stumbling feet, but allow me to be ever near to bind up their bruises."

PERMISSIVENESS

Unqualified permissiveness does not seem to get parents anywhere. There are two kinds of freedom for either a child or an adult, for anyone for that matter, the freedom to do as you please and the freedom to do what you ought. The permissiveness which characterized parental attitudes of the past decade often resulted in juvenile anarchy. A child who all his younger years has been permitted to do as he pleased grows up to discover that the world will not adapt itself to that practice. Parents who act as though there are no rules to the game leave youngsters with no reason to obey.

Further, being permissive is based on the false assumption that a child is born with the capacities for proper choice-making as well as with sound ethical insights. The small child cannot understand the drives that propel him toward waywardness, the perils of materialistic motivation, or on the other hand, the rare meaning of self-denial or even the reasons that are basic to the very rules that he is expected to obey. Such understanding is a matter of growth. A part of this growth is the discovery of the law of cause and effect—a discovery that comes pretty largely through the trial and error of experience. The intent of the parent who is permissive is to circumvent all this and enable the child to escape the pain of facing up to the consequences of his own acts. Only by accepting the principle of doing what one ought and the corollary of facing the consequences of what one does can a child really grow. Thus, growth depends upon true freedom which in turn depends upon rules, rules on order and order on authority.

OVERCORRECTION

But oversupervision and overcorrection can also be harmful. They stunt the creative spirit and genius of the child. They also stunt the growth of the emotional life. It was Faith Baldwin who said, "If you fashion a crutch for someone, he may use it all his life. Many parents have forever crippled their children by an oversupply of 'crutches.'" "You fathers," Paul said, "must not goad your children to resentment, but give them the instruction, and the correction, which belong to a Christian upbringing" (Eph. 6:4 NEB). The Phillips translation reads, "Fathers, don't overcorrect your children." Evidently Paul was against the heavy parental touch. The better procedure for parents is to combine freedom with guidance. As one little girl said, "They want me to do what they want their way, when I want to do what we want my way." Dr. Galen Ross put it this way, "Any home is a good home, if children are taught to behave themselves and mind their manners, and accomplish this priceless result without neglect or physical abuse. It still makes sense to make children mind."

THE CASUAL TOUCH

The more relaxed parent who deals with the little crises of childhood in a casual way seems to get on quite well. You can be as serious as you like when your children kick over the traces, but don't keep rubbing it in. Phyllis McGinley found out that arguing with her eight-year-old daughter about some childish mistake caused her girl to say, "Oh, mommie, why don't you just tell me not to, and stop explaining at me?" Lengthy explanations about an already understood situation or misdemeanor do little good.

Truistic as it may sound, don't nag, don't goad—it's a dead giveaway. You have lost 60 percent of the encounter at the start. If you are going to punish your child, do it without pontification or pampering. In cases of minor dereliction or in instances of continuous neglect, keep cool and be casual. It's the best approach.

UNCONDITIONAL LOVE

The absence of parental love at any one time spells uncertainty to the child. There is a feeling of unreliableness about everything when love is even temporarily suspended. "Mother won't love you if you do that" is a kind of miserable blackmail. In other words, the child will have his parents' love if he meets their requirements. It is precisely when the child is disobedient, does not conform, that he needs the parents' love. Love cannot be intermittent without disastrous effects. There is not much difference between this unfortunate practice and the parental method of correction by the use of force. Henry Guntrip tells of a father and mother and small son who shared his train compartment. The boy became restless,

whereupon his mother said, "If you're not good a man will come and take you away." Just then the engine emitted a shrill whistle and the child started and looked frightened. The father said, "There, that happened because you're not a good boy." Later on, in moving around, the boy put his hand on my knee and the father said, "Take your hand off the gentleman's knee. If you do that he'll pick you up and carry you away." The child darted a quick scared glance at me and was not wholly reassured by my smile.

The principal of a kindergarten told little children in her care that God loves them even when they are naughty. She said that as a result "parents kept calling me to object that I am undermining the discipline of the home." Obvious as it is, we need to be reminded of the fact that parental love is the basic factor in wholesome and normal child development. The prodigal son's father loved his son unconditionally. This fact worked on the son's conscience. The memory of a love that never took a holiday propelled him to turn home. Love is not an extra—love is a stable necessity. Love is not optional, not an adornment. More than a means to happiness, love is an essential—the bread of life.

Babies who are well cared for in every other way in orphanages and foundling homes, have been known to waste away and die without love. In Pearl Buck's book *Letter from Peking* the heroine worked for awhile in a foundling home.

Bed and crib lay side by side, rooms full of children who had been deserted and betrayed. . . . At night I was often waked by the dreadful sound of their weeping. . . . For when a child moaned in her sleep she murmured "mother" and the word waked every child, one and then another, and they wailed the word aloud, "mother—mother." Their crying pervaded the night air and woke other rooms of lonely children until the whole building trembled with the voices of sorrowful children weeping for mothers they could not remember or had never known.

This unconditional love, undeterred, unqualified, ought to be characteristic of the father as well as the mother. Fathers are not exempt from this affectional responsibility.

THE PARENTAL PUSH

It would seem that Paul was looking right at us when he said, "Fathers, do not provoke your children, lest they become discouraged" (Col. 3:21). "Fathers, do not exasperate your children, for fear they grow disheartened," is the New English Bible version. It is hard to understand why Paul did not include both parents in his admonition. We are here interpreting "provoking" in terms of pressure.

THE ABOLITION OF CHILDHOOD

In Charles Dickens' day there was no childhood; children became adults overnight. The growing industrial age banished childhood. The early years faded out into a kind of child-adult existence, grim, forbidding, and traumatic. Today we are abolishing childhood but on different grounds and with different motivation.

A short time ago the writer learned that in Korea families —mother and the children—move into the city of Seoul while the father remains at his work at home. The family thus lives on in separation for years, all in the interest of sending the child to a name school in Seoul. Children in Korea are at their studies from 6:30 in the morning until 11:00 at night. School classes last from 8:30 to 4:00, but the rest of the time is occupied in attending extra classes where the children are tutored in groups, and in study at home where the prodding goes on with every relative taking part. The child must pass the sixth grade with high marks. Pushed by the fear of failing, the child slaves at his studies to get into the middle school and then into college. The emotional strain of this experience is tremendous. Not a few of these children, out of fear of letting down their parents, commit suicide.

For more than half the children in one of our public schools who had been apprehended in cheating, parental pressure for good grades was a contributing factor. In America, while primarily the parental push is on for grades, parents are just as active in coercing their children to get ahead in social life and sports. Children become junior pushers and start pressuring themselves. Schools pitch in and do their part. Dr. Benjamin Spock, whose name is magic in so many households, is against loading school children with extensive homework. In fact, he is even against paying undue attention to scholastic achievement.

But the pressure is on. Girls who should still be playing with dolls are going to dances.

Martha Lear tells us that at a dancing class for children these youngsters were introduced to one another in the following fashion: "Miss Fillmore," says the instructor, "may I present Master Whittaker?" "How do you do," says Miss Fillmore, age seven, languidly extending a white-gloved palm. Miss Lear tells of a group of eleven-year-olds recently booking an eight-way conference telephone call to extend birthday felicitations to a sixth-grade colleague.

We are robbing our children of their childhood. American parents are being seized by a malady infecting them with a horribly distorted kind of child concern—an inordinate interest in their children not for themselves as persons, but for what they as children can achieve in a highly competitive society and what they can gain for the family prestige.

In his first Epistle to the Corinthians, Paul said, "When I became a man I put away childish things." But becoming an adult is a process. Children do not become adults by aping them.

This coercing of children by parents is a part of the jet tempo of our times. Everything is done faster, younger. The pushing of children by parents in its more intense aspects becomes alarmingly harmful. Good will and happiness in the parent-child relationship become dependent upon the child's success in scholarship, athletics, or in social life.

The main parental concern is for a high I.Q. In this is the alpha and omega of social esteem for many parents. An I.Q. tester reports that one woman complainingly said, "I just can't understand it. All of my friends' children are in the 99th percentile. What's the matter with my children?" This threat of pressure to normal healthy childhood offers a very interesting study in the realm of motivation. What is back of all this parental push? Are parents turning to their children as the last best bet for the achievement of status that they themselves could never attain? Is this a new kind of vicariousness in which parents live, strive, and gain a larger place in the sun through the accomplishments of their offspring? Is it because we are caught in a vortex of forces of a youth cult? Or is it because adults find that in their world at the age of forty-five they are no longer desirable in the economic field? Is this realization having a psychological effect motivating them to see everything in terms of getting ahead? Do parents push their children into larger, more ample adult spheres simply because of their own sense of inadequacy? Are people more and more in our society coming under the complete sway of what people will think? All the other families in the neighborhood do this. One person's comment is appropriate at this point, "Too many of us worry about what people think of us when they don't."

The plain tragedy of the abolition of childhood comes at the point of robbing them of the rich and priceless experiences of growing up. Persons, like fruit, ought to ripen. As a result of these parental pressures, children develop guilt feelings, fears and dread, and in some instances those who are extrovert develop a social swagger that makes them almost distasteful. Some of these children simply haven't the capacities to perform on the level into which they are being forced. Too many of our children have grown "discouraged"—"disheartened."

Girls are growing older, younger, all the time, was the judgment of a teenage magazine writer. They are. Girls go steady at thirteen; some fourteen million of them are engaged by seventeen years of age; one-half million girls age fifteen to eighteen are wives, and many of these are mothers. The tragedy is that half the teenage marriages break down.

The devastation of young persons as a result of the social system of the present is in the realm of the emotional life.

Coming as a consequence of parental pressures, many of these youngsters develop dwarfed concepts of life and, given a few years, are inclined to grow bitter and cynical about the whole social system.

SELF-IMAGE

Paul is really saying that when punishment is both cruel and belittling, when reprimand is too severe, "when you over-correct your children—they will grow up feeling inferior and frustrated."

Adult attitudes working in an adult setting are mainly responsible for the kind of self-image that grows in the consciousness of a child. This self-image is of the greatest significance.

Somerset Maugham once put it this way, "When we come to judge others, it is not by ourselves that we judge them, but by an image we have formed of ourselves." "The child is raised in the family whether broken or intact," says Morris Rosenberg. "He may have brothers or sisters in varying combinations; he has parents who have certain feelings toward him; from this ferment of social interaction a self picture begins to emerge." The child feels good about life; life beckons, and he confidently responds; he feels he can make a go of it. If he has a positive self-image life is self-affirming; it instills in the child a love for living; he feels that it is good to be alive, good to be a little boy. With a negative self-image a child feels unsure about himself, uncertain of the estimate of others; he doubts his own abilities; he feels inferior.

The moral or social deformity of a child proceeds from a deformed subjective feeling about the self. It is difficult to understand how deep are the wounds of childhood. One person writes,

Can you help me understand myself? All my life I have been inclined to be melancholy. . . . As a quite small boy I once told my mother I wished I had never been born. Several times I have considered suicide. . . . Ours was a somewhat puritanical home. Father was strictly moral, but not very lovable. He demanded unquestioning obedience of us children. Mother was not so strict, and there were unpleasant scenes between them. Little sentiment was displayed in our family, and I was ashamed to show any myself. . . . Fear played an important part in my earlier days. I was afraid of my father, afraid of storms and death. Mother would show fear when a bad cloud was coming up. This so frightened me, I sometimes hid under the bed. . . . I feel my confusion is growing. A sense of futility and melancholy haunt me. . . . Why do I have such an unnatural slant on life?

Every child has a right to a citadel of adequacy, of self-competence from which to look out on life. "We see that the self-image is never only a self-image," says Daniel Williams, "it is an understanding of life." He goes on to say, "I mean that in the depth of our self-searching we cannot avoid coming upon the ultimate religious questions—what is life? what makes all the pain and struggle worthwhile?"

The most fundamental necessity for the growing child is the development of a sound and healthy feeling of worth that is not on one hand a matter of disruptive individualism or on the other a clinging overdependence. A child needs to have self-esteem, an estimate of himself that comes from the fact that he has a healthy emotional life. This self-estimate should enable him to come to terms with life, to pray for strength and not just a way of escape, to remain teachable, to be able objectively to measure his own capacities, to be able to come to sound decisions based upon the total facts.

THE IMPORTANCE OF THE SELF-IMAGE

Why is the self-image so vital to the growing child? The fact is that the nature and quality of self-confidence reinforced with faith in God and pervaded with an undeniable sense of well-being shapes the inner life of the child. Out of it all there comes a positive incentive for the growing life; telling a lie is robbed of its allure, stealing becomes uninteresting, cheap conduct is seen as uncontributive to the goal of a happy, useful existence. The self-image is related not just negatively to what you do not do, but creatively to a life of positive good.

But how does a child achieve this self-image? Certainly it doesn't just move into his mind. A child grows a self-image by the way he thinks others feel about him. "The child's character may be formed less, the psychologists lead us to believe, by the injunctions and commandments of the parents," says H. Richard Niebuhr, "than by the child's interpretation of the attitudes such commandments are taken to express."

The good-life concept is more common among youth whose parents are on a sound basis maritally and who take a lively and healthful interest in all that youth does. This good-life concept is also found in the child who has had a close relationship with his parents.

The need that all of us have is for acceptance. Here is the key to normality and to a healthy self-image. To be able to accept ourselves because others, mainly our own loved ones, have accepted us—all this combines to give one the ability to accept life and whatever happens in it.

Make no mistake about it, children need to be respected and trusted and, above all, to be loved. Given a satisfying feeling of belonging and family conditions that help build a healthy and helpful self-image, the child has a good chance of growing into strong and useful adulthood.

✤
8. HOUSE

The house and the church have always been in close spiritual proximity. Luke wrote about the new Christians, "And daily in the temple, and in every house, they ceased not to teach and preach Jesus Christ" (Acts 5:42 KJV). The preaching and teaching went on in both church and house; frequently not only worship but the whole life of the church lived on in a home. Paul said, "Give my greetings to Prisca and Aquila, my fellow-workers in Christ. . . . Greet also the congregation at their house" (Rom. 16:3, 5 NEB). Paul also wrote to Philemon from his prison cell, greeting his dear friends "and the congregation at your house" (1:2 NEB).

In the first century churches began in houses. The sanctuary was the house. There the followers of Jesus came to worship, there the new converts received their instruction, there the poor were cared for. There it was that religious faith was inspired, fellowship enriched, and hearts ignited to go out and work for Christ—all this took place in the homes of early Christian leaders. The New Testament speaks of "the House Church." If we are to take the New Testament serious-ly, we may need to weigh the value of starting churches all over our land in the dwelling of committed Christians. The church begins that way out in Hong Kong. Here a Chinese pastor is settled in "a flat" in a multiple-dwelling building. People living in resettlement buildings in close proximity to this flat are invited to worship in this pastor's home. This is how the church begins. The home, along with the experiences that have about them the nature of the ultimate—here is the setting in which religious life can be practiced with lasting effect upon character and faith.

Dr. Leonard Griffith of City Temple, London, describes just such a contemporary "House Church."

This remarkable home belonged to a layman in one of my congregations,—a man who with his wife had been deeply affected by the Oxford Group in its earlier days. In response to his repeated invitations, I went one evening to conduct Bible study for a group that gathered in this home each week. To my utter astonishment I found the place packed, every chair and every inch of the floor occupied by young people between the ages of 20 and 35. We discussed a Bible passage, some of them prayed out loud, and others gave their Christian testimony. I was struck by the composition of the group, which included debutantes, university graduates, and factory hands, some of whom said they could not remember when they last attended a formal church service.

Dr. Griffith goes on to say that people broken in life and character came to that home and found shelter and friendship, as well as material assistance. The father in that home said, "When my wife and I accepted Christ, we asked him, 'Lord, what would thou have us to do?' and we seemed to hear Him saying—'Give me your home. Place it at my disposal and let me use it,' and he has used it to his own glory."

THE CHURCH HELPING THE FAMILY

To establish the "House Church" will not be easy. It necessitates a revolution in the conceptualization of the church. It

98

necessitates a change of focus on the part of organized religion. While we need this change, it may be difficult to accomplish it. We are talking about a change in the relation of the church to the home.

For too long we have thought of the family only in terms of recruits for church membership or support for its program. We have thought in terms of what the family could do for the church. Why not challenge people in our communities to become Christian members of their homes, this being more important than becoming Christian members of the church?

In the past our promotional efforts and our literature, our crusades and our evangelistic meetings, have been aimed at the target of increased church membership. Our basic concern has been to see people through to the Christian life and thus into church membership. Our answer to the dilemma of the family swamped with trouble or conditioned to irreligion has usually been the church service. This in itself is commendable but often grossly insufficient to accomplish the change to Christian family living with its ennoblements.

We are not getting on too well in the church mainly because we have not realized that the most important phases of the work of Christianization cannot be done by the church or the church school alone. Churches that have awakened to this fact are making real progress by adoping a family-centered approach in a family-centered program. Let the church work to establish the Christian life in the home and help maintain it. If this is done, there will be no question as to the support the family will in turn give the church.

We in the church for the most part have worked remote from the family in the home. We know very little about the families that reside in our communities. We may know that a family owns a boat, keeps a dog, has a built-in T.V., is civic-minded and socially important. But we do not know how the members of a family feel about God, whether when trouble comes they know how to fall back on their faith. In the Gospel record we read that Jesus "left the synagogue, and entered the house" (Mark 1:29). This is symbolically the true order—from the church on the corner to the family down the street.

HOUSE SCHOOL

The church can preach, exhort, hold workshops, and install new finance systems, but its real job is to make sure that parents are equipped, disciplined, and dedicated to become co-teachers with those who instruct in the church school, helping them apply spiritual and ethical truth to daily life, and aiding them to mature their spiritual life and characters.

In the Old Testament we read,

And these words, which I command thee this day, shall be in thine heart: and thou shalt teach them diligently unto thy children, and shalt talk of them when thou sittest in thine house, and when thou walkest by the way, and when thou liest down, and when thou riseth up. And thou shalt bind them for a sign upon thine hand, and they shall be as frontlets between thine eyes. And thou shalt write them upon the posts of thy house, and on thy gates" (Deut. 6:6-9 KJV).

If we could carry on a religious life in the home in that fashion —no—unless we do carry on a religious life in the home in that fashion, we will lose the new generation. As far as Christian character is concerned, the church can never do what parents must do. Parents need to say with the psalmist, As for me I will be talking of thy worship, thy glories, thy praise, and wondrous works (Ps. 145:5 KJV).

What we mean by spiritual nurture is indigenously a home affair. This cannot be changed. One can understand Ardis Whitman's statement that it is "as hard for parents today to tell their children about God, as it was for the parents of yesterday to tell theirs about sex." One survey indicates that 98 percent of the million adults questioned were in favor of religious instruction in the home, but many of them did not know where to begin. The great advantage of teaching religion in the home is that the teaching can be identified immediately with the practice of the very truths that are taught. This makes for a maturing into fine Christian manhood and womanhood.

HOUSE OF PRAYER

Perhaps the greatest religious school in the world is a father and mother and a child at prayer. With the decision of the Supreme Court the prayer life of a child has become almost exclusively the responsibility of the home. Too frequently in the modern home the children are put to bed by the baby-sitter, relegating the evening prayers of the children to chance. The priceless experience of hearing their children's prayers is forfeited. More than that, the feeling of security on the part of the child together with the needed spiritual conditioning that comes about when parents pray with their children at the bedside—all this is surrendered. It is precisely at that evening hour that a child is more poignantly sensible to God's care and love. The parents of a small boy informed him that he was old enough to sleep in the dark. The first night, however, he plaintively asked his mother, "Must I sleep in the dark, mummy?" "Yes, darling," she replied. "You are getting to be a big boy now." "Well," was the reply out of the darkness, "may I get up and say my prayers over again—more carefully?"

THE HOUSE CHURCH

The home is a church in the sense of witness—the witness of what you are. "I write this . . . to let you know how men ought to conduct themselves in God's household, that is, the church of the living God." (I Tim. 3:15 NEB.) Jesus ordered a certain man who had been miraculously cured and cleared of an evil spirit, "Return to thine own house, and shew how great things God hath done unto thee" (Luke 8:39 KJV). Jesus urged him to go back home and tell his people about what God had done for him. We need to return to our homes and there to witness to our families concerning what God has done for us. A sense of responsible witness in the home on the part of committed Christians redeems the home from being just a place of convenience. Let the church summon parents to establish the real home—the spiritual home —the home not made with hands. The real home is something other than the size of the lot and the cost of the building. We should be able to say that "the house which I build is great: for great is our God" (II Chr. 2:5 KJV). James Ellenwood constructed a motto to be hung on the walls of his home. The motto was this, "We own this place and it is never going to own us."

The "House Church," a fellowship of Christians in the intimate setting of the home, is the answer to the spiritual need of our day.

❖

9. SPIRIT

The association of the doctrine of the Holy Spirit with family life is in keeping with the recent trend in theological thought and statement.

The writers in this field are concerned to identify the Holy Spirit with objective human experience. In his current book, *Spirit, Son and Father,* Henry Van Dusen says, "The beliefs of our religion when most needed are unshaken, but they do not generate effective power. There is a gap between the convictions in our minds and their grip upon our lives. Faith and practice fail to mesh." The need for an actual experience of the Holy Spirit is squarely before us. Family life offers a prime opportunity for that experience. The Bible has been called with pardonable exaggeration "the Book of the Spirit," but unless the Holy Spirit becomes actual in our lives the whole subject remains doctrinal and academic. "No farmer plows his land by turning it over in his mind." The Holy Spirit must break through into life—must become more than a doctrine.

The Holy Spirit, spoken of by one scholar as the stepchild of theology, has been an awkward subject at the best for most of us. To refer again to Dr. Van Dusen's book, he says that "the Holy Spirit has been for me a late discovery—all early associations in my mind connected with the term were not only vague, but unpleasant, indeed almost repellent." To speak of Spirit today is to indulge in mystification for most people. As one writer says, for some people "it reduces God to an oblong blur."

What is the Holy Spirit? What do we know about it? Is the Holy Spirit similar in its immanence to the Quaker idea of mysticism? Does it bear any likeness to Emerson's concept of inner light? Or is it so general in meaning and nature as to be distinguished only as nonphysical? Many of us do not know what to do with it. The Holy Spirit is that which binds men to God. The Holy Spirit is the spirit of God manifesting itself in the life of mankind everywhere.

Dr. Van Dusen suggests, "A silent, receptive, expectant, consciousness is necessary to the most favorable condition for the disclosure of the Holy Spirit." How is this favorable condition to be obtained in the instance of the family? In view of the fact that the average modern home is as full of turbulence as a disorganized anthill, one wonders how the Holy Spirit is to find even a moment of such propitious circumstance. Speaking of turbulent families, there is that story— it may be apocryphal—of Samuel Wesley, the father of John Wesley, thrown into jail for unpaid debts. Susannah, his wife, carefully going over their household goods, decided to sell some of the furniture to pay the necessary thirty pounds for his release. Leaving her large brood of children she went to visit Samuel in prison to tell him of her intention. We are told that when he heard of her plan he exclaimed, "No, no, Sukey, don't do it! This is the first time I have had any peace."

The family is aided vastly by the work of the Holy Spirit. The family may be spoken of as a community of the Holy Spirit. The Holy Spirit works within this interrelationship.

It is the family that offers a singular setting for its presence and work. We are reminded that it was in the home of John Mark that tradition places the emergence of the Holy Spirit—in tongues of flame to be sure, but nevertheless an unmistakable and historical emanation of the Spirit.

SOME INTERESTING PARALLELS

The physical birth into the human family offers the analogy of spiritual birth into the fuller and more continuous life. "That which is born of the flesh is flesh, and that which is born of the spirit is spirit." Both Matthew and Luke declare that through the Holy Spirit Mary became the bearer of the Christ. (Matt. 1:20; Luke 1:35).

Look at this parallelism further. The Athanasian Creed affirms, "The Godhead of the Father, of the Son, and of the Holy Ghost, is all one." Here is a oneness similar to that in which members of the family, as equal in meaning and value, partake together in a family entity. This family entity is unique. There is a constellation of persons within the Trinity and a constellation of persons within the family.

THE HOLY SPIRIT AND THE UNIVERSAL ORDER

Insight concerning an order that will never pass is a gift of the Spirit. The Spirit makes clear an eternal order that when recognized and accepted becomes the authoritative order for family living. Man has been plagued with disorder, and he is caught in a world in which impermanence stares out at him at every turn. It is in the family that he instinctively senses the presence of an order and a permanence which his soul desires. One of the implications of that order is a moral rightness that does the judging in the instance of each family member's behavior. This order when realized within the family becomes the basis of authority for all its members. This order within the family through the help of the Holy Spirit mirrors an order that is eternal with its resultant sureness about immortality. Working together, hoping together, praying together, believing together—this is a hallowed relationship that will never pass.

THE FAMILY UNDER THREAT

The thing about the family that is threatened by our modern life is its cohesion. Forces emerging from the industrial revolution have brought a new kind of devastation to the home: anonymity with its shrinking of personal worth; moral relativism with its downgrading of standards and its offbeat consequences of intemperance, sexual license, desertion, and divorce; secularism with its shallow goals of the good life.

There are numerous other threats to the solidarity of the family. Father's preoccupation with business and civic affairs has worked its own peculiar deterioration of the home. Too many fathers have abdicated their responsibilities. Father needs to be brought back into the home. While we are about it we may need to bring mother back also. The increasing number of mothers away at work is proving a psychological hazard to the development of child life. Further note the fragmentation of the family due to the multiple interests of its members in community activities. These realizations are brought into an awareness through the work of the Holy Spirit.

One of the real threats to be found is the way in which we take the home for granted. The home needs to be rescued from an unthinking acceptance. We have had centuries to grow accustomed to the home—and we have. The family may be as simple and commonplace as the living room, but it is cosmically wide in its influences. Many of us have preconceived ideas as well as prejudices and feel that there is nothing new to learn about the family. But remove the layers of familiarity and you will come upon the shining truth of its pricelessness. When the Spirit has its way, the wonders and mysteries of life with our loved ones become vivid and real to us.

THE WORK OF THE HOLY SPIRIT IN FAMILY LIFE

The Holy Spirit offers precisely the enablement that the family needs. It is at the juxtaposition of the deteriorations the family suffers and the opportunities the family offers that the Holy Spirit can accomplish its greatest work.

The Holy Spirit provides the needed dynamic for the enrichment of interpersonal relations of the family. How can the coherent life of the family, rich in understanding, tolerance, and love, be sustained? Paul told the Galatians, "But the fruit of the Spirit is love, joy, peace, patience, kindness, goodness, faithfulness, gentleness, self-control" (5:22-23). To sustain these high and holy qualities in family life is the work of the Holy Spirit. Paul goes on to say, "If we live by the Spirit, let us also walk by the Spirit" (Gal. 5:25).

In effecting man's fulfillment the Holy Spirit can best work through the experience of marital relations, parenthood, and the growing life. The Holy Spirit moves persons to live according to God's plan. "And I will put my spirit within you, and cause you to walk in my statutes, and ye shall keep my judgments, and do them." (Ezek. 36:27 KJV.)

The consideration of the Holy Spirit must certainly come to life at the point of man's instinctual nature: the attraction of the sexes for each other, the fulfillment in sexual love, the procreation of new life, the sense of vocation in the family venture, the tyrannical father, the possessive mother, the husband or wife whose ego demands are getting out of hand. "Live your whole life in the Spirit and you will not satisfy the desires of your lower nature. For the whole energy of your lower nature is set against the Spirit, while the whole power of the Spirit is contrary to the lower nature." The Holy Spirit works in family life, prompting each member to bring the expression of his emotional needs up to the concept of the divine meaning of others within the home. The work of the Spirit will give guidance to husband and wife in the experiences of their sexual love. Without this guidance nothing can save us from affectional bankruptcy and marital dissolution. Human love in its inevitable erotic element needs the discrimination as well as the sanctification of the Spirit.

The Holy Spirit works at the heart of life, in the midst of its intimacies and its inner struggle. "The distinctive characteristics of the idea of 'spirit,'" said Van Dusen, "are intimacy and potency." It is precisely this in-depth activity of the Spirit that is needed. The problems of marriage and the family are in-depth problems. The Holy Spirit works within a person and within a relationship to awaken the life to the fact that God strengthens and Christ controls. It is in depth that a family is in conflict, carries on its struggles, experiences its emotional hungers—it is at this very depth of intimacy and of finality that the Holy Spirit comes with power to lead the life of the home to trust God and to thus find the answer.

One thing more, the function of the Holy Spirit is to heal and comfort. "I will not leave you comfortless," Jesus says. "I will come unto you"—and he does, in the form of the Holy Spirit. Where better can the Holy Spirit do its comforting work than in the family?

The doorway to the home is the doorway through which the miraculous Spirit of God enters and empowers each member of the family to holy living. The Holy Spirit can energize the family at its heart, establish a climate of spiritual hoping and seeking. This prompting, alerting, igniting work of the Holy Spirit, like the needle of a compass, brings the family through to what is Christian.

The Holy Spirit as a spiritual presence nourishes incentive and hope within a family, encourages these impulses toward the holy. It turns the dismal prospect into possibilities of great good. These are the experiences of the family, as God is revealed in the life of it, through the Holy Spirit. This is the creative work of the Spirit. In the upper room before leaving his disciples, Jesus said, "The Helper, the holy Spirit whom the Father will send in my name, will teach you everything and recall to you everything I have said" (John 14:26 Moffatt).

Take this engoldening experience of the family beginning with two young persons—an awakened love, the marriage vow, the bearing of hopes and fears, the immeasurable dependence of the child's heart—if in all these steps of the familial way we can know the presence of the Holy Spirit, we shall experience the true growth of soul and personality. Suggesting, counseling, revealing—so shall the Spirit lead us as families to God's great mercy and to the fullness of life in Christ Jesus.

THE SPIRIT BRINGS THE GLORY

The Spirit brings to the home an experience of glory— "a glory full of grace and truth." The windows of the home become the windows of heaven. "The Spirit will glorify me," said Jesus, "he will take what is mine and declare it to you." How can a family have this fulfilling glory? By repenting of its self-centeredness and its idolatry of mammon, by becoming sensitive to the power of the Holy Spirit and living the Christ way.

It is in the relationship of the family that "God hath wrought great glory"; it is there that one finds the joys of an assuring memory, the touch of a thoughtful act that will live again in reflection, the courage of passing through the dark valley together, the respect that cannot be dislodged by misfortunate or regrettable behavior. This is the flame of life and love through which the Spirit moves and does its work.

Through these family relationships, luminous and eternal, the Spirit shines. And so at last we end where we began— at home in our homes with God, reconciled by the Christ, guided by the Holy Spirit, brought back to our Creator-Father.

F